The Second Wave

Transcending the Human Drama

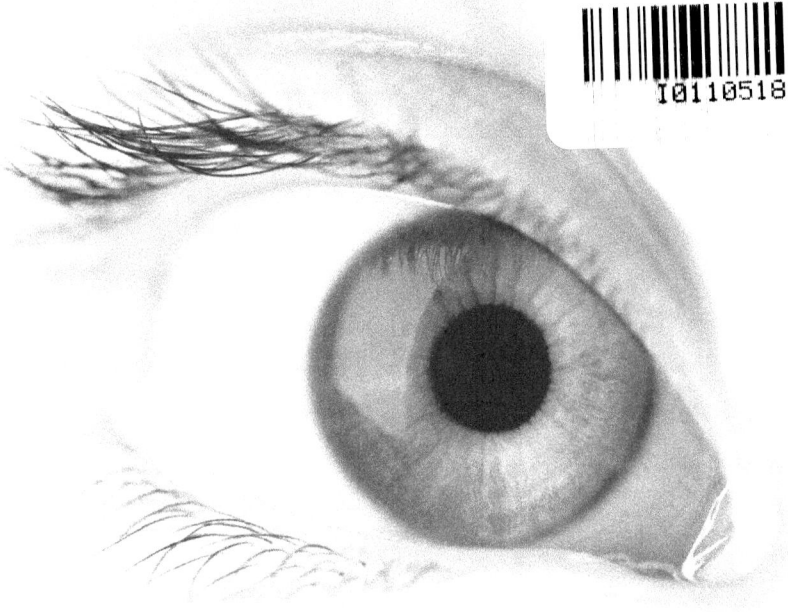

I0110518

White Eagle

expressed through my muse and daughter

Kerri Hummingbird Sami

with contributions from
Lisa Barnett, Jennifer Hough and Gary Stuart

First published in the United States of America by Siwarkinte Publishing

The Second Wave: Transcending the Human Drama
Kerri Hummingbird Sami channeling White Eagle

Cover design by © Kerri Hummingbird Sami
Illustration by © Kerri Hummingbird Sami
Photograph of Kerri Hummingbird Sami by The Perfect Headshot
Photograph in cover artwork by ID 20012003 © Elena Elisseeva I Dreamstime.com

This book may be ordered directly from Amazon.com.

ISBN-13: 978-0-578-53018-5

For more information about Kerri Hummingbird, visit:
Web: www.kerrihummingbird.com
Twitter: @KerriHummingbrd
Facebook: Kerri.Hummingbird
Instagram: kerri.hummingbird
Pinterest: kerrihummingbrd
YouTube: Kerri Hummingbird

Praise for *The Second Wave* by Kerri Hummingbird

As someone who's clearly walked the path, Kerri now leads us to a Divine reality—the new earth that is ours to create. Her deep understanding of shamanic and spirit wisdom helps us climb out of the karmic collective consciousness and move to our rightful place as sovereign souls. Wise, insightful and eminently useful for the spiritual seeker!

— Sara Wiseman, Author of *Messages from the Divine* and *The Intuitive Path*

The author, Kerri Hummingbird, shares with honesty and heart-warming courage her journey into what it means to be a human being who is awake and in conscious action. If you want to discover who you are, what you are and what is next then read Kerri's book. I am going to continue to open this book to remember the encyclopedic insight and supportive suggestions of what's possible in creating a meaningful, joy-filled life for ourselves and for future generations.

—Dr. Anita L. Sanchez, International Award Winning and Best Selling Author, Speaker, and Trainer of *The Four Sacred Gifts: Indigenous Wisdom for Modern Times*

If you have ever suspected you are part of something bigger, *The Second Wave* is just the book you are looking for. While we can often think that change on the planet, and in human evolution, is down to someone else, this book explores why it is incumbent on each of us to be a harbinger of that change. The Second Wave is so needed right now when our so-called leaders seek to spread fear and divide. This book is all about us coming together for our collective benefit. While short in size, it is big in concept.

— Tom Evans, Insight Timer Meditation Guide and Author of *Soulwaves: A Future History*

A resounding and joyful "hallelujah!" for this long-awaited and much-needed guide for healers and lightworkers. The "Second Wave" brings relief, clarity, understanding and comfort to all souls who have struggled throughout this lifetime. It's a true healing balm. Kerri Hummingbird beautifully channels Divine wisdom that will profoundly shift your perception, provide you with easy to implement practices and enable you to finally embrace your light and step more fully into your reason for being on this planet. You came here to make a difference and with this book as your companion, you finally can! Bravo!

— Lisa Winston, #1 International Bestselling Author of *Your Turning Point* and Co-host of *The Mindset Reset Show*

We live in an ego based society where outward success and left brained focus is the most rewarded and recognized. Historically, this has left many light workers, empaths, highly sensitive people, right brain creators and powerful healers in the world feeling they don't belong and their gifts aren't worthy. This couldn't be further from the truth as Kerri Hummingbird so eloquently outlines in her newest book, *The Second Wave*. She is a messenger of the words your soul needs you to hear because the time has come in the world where light leaders are the appointed and most needed to take the helm during the Second Wave to create an accelerated evolution in human consciousness. Her words are a balm to your being if you ever wondered what your place is in the world. Not only does she describe the thoughts, feelings, actions and needs of a Second Wave leader, she also gives practical and useful tools for your own healing and evolution. This is a must read now if you know deep inside your soul is calling you to use your natural born gifts as a light leader and play a bigger role in world transformation.

— Debbie Lynn Grace, Transformational Leader, Energy Worker, Intuitive and Author of *Outrageous Business Growth*

A beautiful inspiring must-read book! Not since "Eat, Pray, Love" have I enjoyed reading a book so much. Full of beautiful stories and wisdom for those who simply know that now is the time to build a new world and we are the ones called to do it.

— Teresa de Grosbois, #1 International Bestselling Author of *Mass Influence - the Habits of the Highly Influential*

Kerri Hummingbird's *The Second Wave* is a beautiful flow of spirit, through her, to you. Her words immediately integrate this divine wisdom into something you can experience and heal with. "To heal something, you must experience it personally. You can't heal other people's stuff. Not really. Even as a healer, we are only holding space for the person to heal themselves." This is a book that takes you on a healing journey that lightens the soul and I am in bliss while traveling it.

— Jacki Smith, Founder of Coventry Creations and Author of *Coventry Magic and DIY Akashic Wisdom*

Kerri offers wonderful stories of her experience with various indigenous shamans. Reading the ideas from these ancient indigenous, as well as their application for helping the world and humanity today, stirs the awakening process in the reader. In addition to sharing helpful insights and quotes, Kerri offers actionable steps for readers to directly experience aligning with spirit and nature for the reader's highest good; such as how to clean your mind-body, and ancestral karma. Thanks Kerri for stepping out of the 'crazy closet' with this book and sharing your light with the world and the rest of us crazy folks.

— Swami Sadashiva Tirtha, Monk, Shaman, Healer, Bestselling Author of the *Ayurveda Encyclopedia*

Kerri's book is different from any other I've read that explores other dimensions. It's a great read, to start. But it's her compassion and appreciation for the human journey — along with a plethora of techniques and perspectives — that reverberates with healing and presence in this world. She helps us to live the life we're here to live and give.

—Sondra Kornblatt, bestselling author of *Restful Insomnia and A Better Brain at Any Age*

"I've encountered so many people in recent months who've said, 'I feel an awakening and I know I'm here for some bigger purpose.' If you feel this calling in your heart or if you've already made the leap to follow it, The Second Wave is a wonderful read to guide you on your soul's celestial journey. What I absolutely love about this book is the way author Kerri Hummingbird beautifully teaches you how to raise the loving vibrations of your mind, body and soul, how to navigate your true purpose and how to connect with the divine while you walk this blessed path."

— Robert Clancy, international bestselling author of *Soul Cyphers: Decoding a Life of Hope and Happiness*

The planet does not need more successful people.

The planet desperately needs more peacemakers, healers, restorers, storytellers, and lovers of all kinds.

—*Dalai Lama*

♥

Darkness cannot drive out darkness; only light can do that. Hate cannot drive out hate; only love can do that.

—*Martin Luther King, Jr.*

♥

There are only two mistakes one can make along the road to truth; not going all the way, and not starting.

—*Buddha*

Acknowledgements

*Thank you to my loving husband Akeem for always believing in me,
supporting my purpose work, and telling me to "bring more, brighter!"
Thank you to my sons Garrett and Tanner for inspiring me to be the best
mother I could through the twists and turns our lives have taken. Thank you
to Yamina and Chi for bringing your light into my life.*

*The wisdom I have delivered in this book was made possible through personal
evolution, facilitated via training with many incredible people, and I have
lots of thanks to give. You have all helped me learn to access the Great Spirit.*

*Thank you to the Q'ero, Huichol, and Shipibo shamans for sharing your
medicine and wisdom and waking me up to Walk the Beauty Way.*

*Thank you to the PowerPath School of Shamanism community, Red Foxes,
Jose and Lena Stevens, and Anna and Aaron Harrington for demonstrating
love and opening me to the most fascinating discovery of all.*

*Thank you to Tracey Trottenberg and George Kansas and our messenger
tribe for helping me own, honor, and unleash my message into the world.*

*Thank you to my Four Winds Light Body School teachers and mentors for
powerful energy medicine and a fresh start in my life including Chris
Prietto, Kris Thoeni, Julie Hannon, Christina Allen, Lynn Berryhill, Peter
Bonaker, Ruby Parker, and Jon Rasmussen.*

*Thank you to HeatherAsh Amara, Diana Adkins, Gerry Starnes, and
Chrispy Bhagat Singh for helping me lift out of darkness into my purpose.*

*Thank you Teresa de Grosbois and the Evolutionary Business Council for
always lifting me up to shine even brighter.*

*Thank you to my mother for making me strong and wise, and pushing me to
know my own truth and stand in it with confidence.*

Thank you to all my guides, ascended masters, and ancestors beyond the veil.

Especially, White Eagle. I love you with all my heart.

♥

Contents

Preface

I'd like to share with you a story of my unfolding with White Eagle. It begins in 2012 with an inner urgency to connect with my indigenous ancestry that was prompted by being re-awakened in this lifetime to the shamanic path by my first teacher, Gerry Starnes. I had been prompted to find a shaman by a conversation I had with a friend shortly after the end of my 20 year marriage. She had mentioned receiving a healing from a shaman that forever changed her life, and so that night I searched the Internet for "shaman in Austin" and found Gerry. His community, The Shamanic Community of Austin, leads drum journey circles weekly. I interviewed for his group mentoring program, was accepted, and within a couple of months received my first shamanic healing. This healing was like the tiny snowball set loose at the top of a giant mountain. The full story of the first two years of my healing journey are chronicled in *Awakening To Me: One Woman's Journey To Self Love* (at the request of my 'guide').

In my quest to find proof of my great-great grandmother's Cherokee heritage, I visited Cherokee Heritage Center and Oconaluftee Indian Village in the Great Smoky Mountains in the summer of 2012. She had changed her name because she could pass for white, which blocked progress finding her in the rolls, but I had hoped there was another way. My quest at this juncture was fruitless, so I continued my work in shamanic drum journey to connect to my ancestry beyond the veil.

In 2014 I revisited the Oconaluftee Indian Village in the Great Smoky Mountains with my sons as we made our way back from my grandmother's funeral on the east coast. This time my request to connect with a medicine man who could help led me to a man who happened to be working the flint arrow demonstration that day. Bruce was touched by my heartfelt tears and deep desire to connect with my ancestry, and said he would meet me after his shift.

Seeing as his shift was almost over, I turned with my sons to walk toward the meeting place when a most amazing thing happened.

A ball of energy the size of a Texas grapefruit was flung into the back of my head where it meets the neck. I now know this is a spiritual gateway called the 'Mouth of God.' I was instantly dizzy and had to sit down. I could see the trees breathing. I talk about this more in "Past Lives, Imprints and Walk-Ins" later in this book. However, what became clear to me was that I now was sharing body/mind/energy space with a Cherokee Chief who had lived heartbreaking suffering of the Trail of Tears.

The next several years while I was completing energy medicine training at the Four Winds Light Body School, and working on advanced trainings with HeatherAsh Amara, I was healing the grief of this Cherokee Chief which was enormous. I came to realize that we were to work together to heal the divide between white people and red people. His heart and my heart became one over time in layers of healing ceremony. Clairvoyants often saw him standing behind me with arms crossed saying "Too many thinking" and shaking his head. He definitely helped me as much as I helped him. He was helping me to reclaim my honor as a woman, and for that I am eternally grateful.

Then in 2016 I went with the Four Winds and Alberto Villoldo to Ausangatay, the Holy Mountain, in Peru. We camped at 14,000 feet for several days as we did ceremony with the Q'ero shamans. On the final day was a hike up to the top to the Rainbow Lagoon. Anyone who could not make the trek to 16,000 feet was urged to stay behind. I knew I needed to go to the Rainbow Lagoon. I also knew I was 47 years old and not as fit as the younger people who were heading up. Alberto poked at my fear the night before, "Kerri, you've had trouble up here at altitude. You should strongly consider not going tomorrow. You don't want the others to have to turn around if you can't make it." I spent all night tossing and turning in my tent, but inevitably, it came down to faith. I trusted Ausangatay to help me get to the Rainbow Lagoon because I knew it was my destiny to do so.

On the hike, which was at points straight up and challenging with lack of oxygen, I saw something the others passed by. It looked like white snow on the ground. I was drawn to it. As I approached, I saw what it was. It was a fallen white eagle lying on the cold ground.

I took some feathers from the end of its wing, and placed them in my backpack. The Q'ero shaman came and collected the rest of the bird when he saw what I had found, and was a bit confused as to why I took the feathers. I just knew that they were for me.

Later in that day back at the hotel, I meditated with the feathers. I had a vision of the Cherokee Chief except this time he told me his name was White Eagle. When I did an Internet search, I found that Cherokee tribes often had White Eagle Chiefs that were the leaders in time of peace. So I assumed that this was a reclaimed part of my soul that had been a Cherokee peace chief on the Trail of Tears. I left it at that in my mind, and looked no further.

At the closing despacho ceremony with the Q'ero shamans, one of the shamans made a statement with a hand gesture towards me. I asked what he said, and my friend translated. "They think you are the Rainbow Keeper." Incidentally, after the trip to Ausangatay was when I started channeling rainbow light during my healing sessions. It's pretty cool channeling rainbow light, and so I was happy.

Then I began doing plant medicine work and having experiences while drumming in ceremony of my Cherokee Chief asking me to let go of the drum stick so he could drum for me. It was a strange feeling to let go of my hand and allow him to drum, and yet it was also relaxing because he could hear the music better than me. So in many ceremonies, we practiced this co-creation of drumming.

Flash forward to October 2017, I was in Lubbock in a morning meditation before driving to Santa Fe to take a healing class with the PowerPath School of Shamanism. It was a really expanded meditation and I could 'hear' the guides beyond the veil discussing my request to do my mission. I'd been saying for years that I was ready, although I did not at the time have any idea what I was to be ready *for*. I just knew I was rearing to go. I heard one of the guides say "She's not ready" and I retorted "Yes I am!". Things seemed to calm and settle and I came out of my meditation and started driving.

Later that day I picked up a friend in Albuquerque and took a call with a radio host who was considering whether to interview me. He had millions of listeners so I was overjoyed when he invited me to be on his show! I hung up the phone exalted and then looked down to see a missed call from my mother. When I called her back I found out the news I never wanted to hear. My Dad was in the hospital with one quarter of a lung functional, an unexpected infection, and I needed to turn around right away.

I drove 15 hours straight to the hospital to arrive at 4am. I curled up by his bedside, and for several hours my Dad and I journeyed together in that thin space between the veils. To the world he was asleep, but he and I were reminiscing about all the wonderful experiences we shared. He reminded me of many things I had forgotten, and would say "I can't believe you forgot that!". It was a beautiful life review with my Dad in the imaginal space of Spirit, and eased my distress that he would leave me behind.

The next morning he took his last breath and with a gush of white light, he was gone from his body. Just like that. As the family gathered around his body holding hands a few hours later, listening to the pastor say a few words for his passing, we started hearing him one by one. First I heard him say it, and it made me smile. Then I saw my brother smiling, and then my son. And I asked them with a giggle, "Can you hear what he's saying?" And they giggled and said "Yes. He wants us to shout 'GRACE!'" This was our family custom at Thanksgiving and Christmas, and admittedly sacrilegious, but we would all hold hands before eating dinner and shout at the top of our lungs, so God could hear us, "GRACE!!"

My Dad was a huge presence in a room. He commanded attention without even trying. He was the most understanding person I've ever met. My family had something special and we kept it all to ourselves. Or tried to. Because no matter where my Dad went, he knew just how to say the silliest thing to make a person smile. I often tried to get time alone with him so we could have spiritual discussion. He had so many profound things to say, and always practical wisdom. He had a way of asking you questions that led you right to the answer you wanted, but without telling you the answer himself. It was amazing, and completely frustrating when you wanted him to cut to the chase.

We all knew that he already knew the answer; he just wanted us to find it for ourselves.

Two weeks after my Dad died I went to a medicine ceremony where I was able to reconnect with him beyond the veil. And I received a healing that integrated a masculine energy with my own which my healer said was "a very big honor." I thought to myself this must be my Dad, and yes, it would be a very big honor to receive his support. In fact, I felt much more supported and stronger after this healing, and was able to make good progress with my business which previously had been challenging.

And so I continued on my healing path through very tumultuous times after my father's passing, and I knew I was being called up to service. Every tough challenge I needed to face was before me to strengthen me. Without my Dad in the family, there were immense shoes to fill. He had been such a powerful force in our family, that I had leaned on him a great deal and been somewhat entitled, even as I liked to think of myself as empowered. His absence focused a bright light on every shadow of our family dynamic...all the places where he had been the compassionate glue preventing eruptions. I had to climb a mountain within myself to become my own support, and to lead my sons toward a better outcome.

At the beginning of 2019 I began receiving downloads that there was big work to do this year, and in February I received the message that I needed to write a new book. "What book am I writing?" I wondered, and then I got the message that I was writing a book for the Second Wave. "What is the Second Wave?" I asked. And then I was guided to look up Dolores Cannon's work, and remembered that along the way I had watched one of her videos about the volunteers to Earth.

More confirmations came from other clairvoyants that I had a 'big mission' on Earth as I began channeling this book from my 'guide'. I still had no idea who the guide was, and there was a lot of back and forth about what to call my 'guide'. In my meditations, my 'guide' and I settled on 'the Great Spirit' which is always accurate since we are all part of the Creator of all that is.

The spring of 2019 was a flurry of channeling for this book along with lots of spiritual development workshops and mentoring to lift me to the place where I could reasonably serve to share the book's messages with others in a believable way. In other words, because I had already walked the path that the book suggests others consider walking. Life conspired to deliver grueling spiritual work to my doorstep as I worked in my own life to close the Book of Fate.

A delightful synchronicity happened where I saw artwork created by Katherine Skaggs, and was immediately drawn to an image of White Eagle. Her rendition captures exactly the feeling that I have of my 'guide' that I have been working with; my White Eagle Chief. Her artwork is designed to create a portal to this ascended master, and I believe procuring my little altar card of his image assisted my awakening greatly.

Still, I had no idea who my 'guide' was until a medicine journey just days before I was planning to print this book. Finally, I was able to break through the Earth amnesia and have the clearest conversation of my life with my 'guide'. He confirmed all my small knowings over years that had slipped past my sight as knowings often do when the ego is involved.

White Eagle chuckled, "They'll never see it coming."

Heck! I never saw it coming. Well, I did. But I didn't believe it. And that's really what happens for so many people on the path. Our souls send clear signs and we brush them away as preposterous because the rational mind doesn't believe it can be. It took being blindsided by plant medicine for me to finally surrender and break through so I could **know** I was born of White Eagle, beyond doubt.

I believe that ascended masters can ethereally guide and even embody multiple people at once. White Eagle showed me many moments where my Dad specifically taught me lessons that would be highly relevant as I entered my direct work with White Eagle. For example, my Dad had a diagnosis of an aggressive cancer years before he died, and he wanted to pursue chemotherapy if it came out of stasis. With my faith in energy medicine, I disagreed and it was causing problems in our relationship. Finally, I relented to simply be a support to my Dad and stopped trying to convince him to try spiritual healing. He said to me "I notice you are now listening. I know you are a strong leader, but this is my life, and I need you to follow." White Eagle reminded me of this moment, and its significance to the relationship between personality and soul, as well as the importance of leaders being able to follow.

This is just one of the many significant moments that White Eagle brought to my attention during ceremony, connecting the dots of my life, and showing me how he had orchestrated everything…including all the many lessons I learned from my Dad (my step-father) from the moment he met me as a little red-headed five year old child on the stoop of the apartment complex where I was living with my mother and first step-father. I wasn't my Dad's biological daughter…I was his soul daughter, and he found me right on time.

I do not pretend to know how White Eagle can be my Dad, and my soul guide, and my Cherokee Chief, and inside me embodied, and talking to you ethereally, and serving you in whatever way he does, and leading the way into the Age of Aquarius. He only tells me what I need to know when I need to know it. He tells me I am his messenger, his muse, his hummingbird, and his daughter. He designed me for the role I am to play, and he mentored me in physical reality too just to be sure I 'got' the lessons I needed.

White Eagle suggested I put his name on the cover to give the book some credibility, and had a hearty laugh. I laughed and agreed. I could use some of that.

May your spiritual journey have as many twists and turns as my own with a mentor as loving, gentle, kind, wise, and supportive as White Eagle.

Things are never as they appear. They're better.

❤

THE SECOND WAVE

Welcome Home

Have you ever walked into a party a few hours late? Everyone has been there talking and drinking and carrying on, and you're the sober one in the room. You quickly try to disguise yourself to blend in, but what's happening around you is not really making sense. *Why are people acting the way they are?* They're clearly under the influence of something that is taking them out of their true nature.

Has your whole life on Earth been this experience? What if the party you've crashed has been going on for thousands of years, and you've just arrived?

Have you always felt like an outsider, a stranger in a strange land? Perhaps you've even been the black sheep of your family? Have you wanted to return home almost since you were born? While everyone else thought a heartless behavior was perfectly fine and seemed impervious, your heart was broken that such a thing could happen....does that sound like you? Have you felt the density and heaviness of humanity, as if you are Hercules lifting everyone around you out of negativity? Maybe you felt like roles were reversed as a child and you were the caretaker?

Your whole life you've been told you're too sensitive and need to get a thicker skin. But accepting the 'way things are' felt like an affront to your inner knowing and integrity. You often feel like you're taking on others' burdens and processing it. You need to regenerate your energy by sequestering yourself in your home like a hermit. Paradox: You feel urgency about remembering your purpose and bringing your light to humanity.

Your life so far may have been pretty bumpy. You've experienced more than your share of tragedies, sometimes all at once. Childhood abuse, emotional neglect, physical attack, abandonment, bullying, illness, accidents, poverty, rape, incest, shame, blame, guilt, judgement. Perhaps you've considered or attempted suicide. Which did you experience? All of the above?

To lift out of the darkness, you've found yourself interested in, even compelled to explore, healing modalities and spirituality and psychology.

You've never felt like you were home on Earth. So I say to you, "Welcome Home." Doesn't that feel good? It means that we reached the point of our mission where the tide is ready to turn and we're going to do what we came here to do. *It's about to get really amazing on Earth.*

Close your eyes and drop your attention to the divine spark in the center of your chest under your heart chakra. Let that divine spark expand its light. Breathe three deep breaths into your divine spark to grow its intensity. Then drop the question down, "Is *<your name>* part of the Second Wave?" Listen for the answer.

If the answer was *Yes*, it means you're a volunteer that chose to come to Earth to help her transition into New Earth. You may be culminating lifetimes on Earth and lending your expertise to this mission. Or you're a being of light from another part of the galaxy, or an Earth-based being of light, that was willing to pull your essence down into a physical human body for the purpose of changing humanity from the inside out.[1]

This was an incredibly generous loving gesture to come to Earth, a planet that has been trapped by cycles of karma into a very slow rate of growth in consciousness. Collectively, GOD decided to intervene to assist Earth in her new transition into the Aquarian age by helping her human creation to elevate consciousness and survive. Planet Earth has gone through five extinctions so far as a result of humanity; the Second Wave is here to prevent the sixth extinction. We have work to do, and it can be an adventure.

Use your preferred word for God: Creator, Source, Universe, Divine, Oneness, Great Spirit. In this text, we will use *Great Spirit*. Great Spirit captures the truth that we are all part of the same infinite consciousness, even as we individuate ourselves with a name, a body, a soul. We all have access to receive messages and guidance from the Great Spirit because we are each created from and a part of the collective consciousness of the Great Spirit. Everything that ever was throughout all time, space and dimension is part of the Great Spirit.

As I am writing this book, I am listening to the Great Spirit[2] for messages to convey to you. Some of these messages I have heard or experienced in my incarnation here on Earth. Some of the messages simply pour onto the page, simultaneously astounding me and reminding me of something I know from another aspect of myself beyond this current lifetime. You are invited to filter all messages conveyed in this text through your own truth meter; access your own connection to Great Spirit and feel yourself as you read…do you feel a resonance or a *knowing*?

You are part of the Great Spirit, and you've lived other lifetimes, potentially in other parts of the galaxy, and right now you are incarnated on Earth and probably remember very little, if any, of your soul history. Why did you forget? Why has it been so hard to remember who you really are? Why have you struggled in confusion?

This is because of *Earth amnesia*. When most beings come to Earth to inhabit a human form, they forget who they really are so they can deeply immerse in the experience of being human in a lifetime. Waking up from the Earth amnesia can take years, with tiny moments of clarity sprinkled through dreams and moments that are later dismissed by the ego as preposterous.

Combine Earth amnesia with karma and free will and you can see why humans on Earth have suffered setbacks in the evolution of consciousness. The karma of every lifetime is embedded in the human DNA and passed down to the next generation, thereby adding more red tape for the incoming souls to clear before making significant progress ascending consciousness.

The suppression of ancient wisdom about epigenetics and recapitulation and healing DNA of ancestral patterns has further enslaved humanity by trapping them in cycles of abuse. A lack of understanding about the power of the Word and creation has led humans to further burden themselves by creating institutions of fear and birthing energetic forms to enforce fear-based thinking in the collective consciousness.

If you look at human history from a bigger perspective, you can see that humans have created structures at all levels to limit themselves to repeat past mistakes from government to education to religion to economics to diet and self-care and beyond into the unseen world that surrounds the planet. The self-loathing and disconnection of humanity is poisoning human bodies, birthing new humans into a system of self-loathing, destroying other forms of life on the planet, and now poisoning the Earth herself.

With New Earth, all of this creation of human suffering comes crumbling down. As I listen to the Great Spirit, I hear that the Second Wave of volunteers has come specifically to experience all of the human viruses of suffering that run through the DNA and to heal it using ancient wisdom, seven generations forward and seven generations back. The Second Wave of volunteers is here to raise their own inner vibrations through this work to elevate consciousness in their own family lines as a top priority. Next priority is to generate the ascended vibrations into their communities. And finally, to guide others as they wake up into the higher consciousness to drop the baggage of past human history so we can collectively evolve.

You are now invited to remember who you are in truth and love, to forgive and release your human history, and to step into service. You've had your human experience, you embodied the patterns of suffering that require healing for humanity to progress, and now is the time to fully heal, forgive and release it from your own body so you can close that old Book of Fate and open the new Book of Destiny you also came here to experience. The Book of Fate can be thought of as the 'I am broken' story; as you close that book, you release the notion that there is something wrong with you that needs to be fixed. As you open the Book of Destiny, a more relevant question is "What is this vessel capable of?" The exploration is to discover all the capabilities of your humanity as you bring your divinity to it. You may very well heal your ancestral DNA and personal life traumas as part of the Book of Destiny, but as you do so, it will be from a space of curiosity, love, discovery, and expansion.

On a personal note, I know deeply how hard it has been. It is so vulnerable to be a sensitive feeling soul on Earth at this time, and many lightworkers have succumbed to the darkness. Up until now, it has been painful to feel like you don't belong, to feel misunderstood, to feel unwanted and unsupported and unappreciated, and to go through so many challenges without anyone around you knowing or understanding the true value of your presence and service. Allow yourself to grieve and witness your pain so you can honor it, and then ask the Winds of the West to release it to the past.

"I know who you are in truth and love.
I know what you are in truth and love.
I know how you serve in truth and love.
You are here, you are here, you are here.
And you are free, you are free, you are free."

(Acknowledging Paul Selig for channeling this mantra
for the benefit of us all.)

Yes…you are as free of your history as you choose to be.

New Earth awaits you. The party has already started, and you are welcomed to it. You have lived much of your life feeling alone and isolated. You are not alone. You are joined by hundreds of thousands of volunteers. Approximately 10% of the population is part of the Second Wave.

The New Earth is dawning. Rejoice!

❤

The Three Waves of Volunteers and

The New Earth (Dolores Cannon)

"So the purpose of the three waves is two-fold. One: to change the energy of the Earth so it can avoid catastrophe. And two: to help raise the energy of the people so they can ascend with the Earth into the next dimension.

The first wave of these souls [...] have had the most difficult time adjusting. They don't like the violence and ugliness they find in this world and want to return 'home' - even though they have no idea, consciously, where that might be. Emotions disturb and even paralyze them especially strong ones like anger and hate. They cannot handle being around people expressing them. These dramatically affect them, as though emotions are foreign to them. They are used to peace and love because that was what they experience where they came from. Even though these people seem to have a good life, loving family and a good job, many of them try to commit suicide. There seems to be no logical reason, yet they are so unhappy they don't want to be here.

The second wave [...] are moving through life much more easily. They are generally focused on helping others, creating no karma, and normally going unnoticed. They have been described as antennas, beacons, generators, channels of energy. They have come in with a unique energy that greatly affects others. They don't have to do anything. They just have to be. I have been told that just by walking through a crowded mall or grocery store their energy affects everyone they come in contact with. It is that strong, and of course, they do not realize this consciously. The paradox is that although they are supposed to be affecting people by their energy, they really don't feel comfortable being around people. So many of them stay home secluded, to avoid mixing with others, even working from their homes. Thus they are defeating their purpose." [3]

Why You Came Here

Earth is in the middle of a transition that will last for 2150 years: the Age of Aquarius. There are lots of debates as to when the transition into the Age of Aquarius actually happens, or whether it already happened as one might suspect from the music and culture of the 1960s. But as I listen to the Great Spirit, I hear the message that the transition formally begins in the year 2020. The 1960s was the time that the First Wave volunteers were active as human adults on Earth, and so that makes sense to me knowing that correlation.

Coincidentally, I had a premonition when I was in high school that the year 2020 was significant in a way that felt so large it provoked a certain fear in my mind that something ominous might happen. From my perspective today, I see that it was simply the huge significance of the transition into the Age of Aquarius that I felt rippling back through time. I did not understand time and how it could ripple and be felt when I was 18 years old.

And for a moment, let's talk about that change in perspective. It has been a change in identity. When I was 18 years old (and for three decades after), I thought I was a human girl planning a life filled with a chosen career, a love partnership, and eventually a marriage with children. I thought I was deciding whether to be a writer or a publicist. I had no idea who I actually was until, decades later, I saw the end of the rope. *Literally.*

I saw a vision of a ships rope knotted at the end, and I saw and felt it get yanked from my open hand. This vision told me very clearly that it was time to leave my 20 year relationship and venture into some unknown destiny that I hoped would produce more fulfillment than I had been experiencing in my karma relationship. The demise of my first marriage was necessary for my evolution and part of my soul plan.

Putting the puzzle together in retrospect, I remember that right before everything blew up in my life, I had visited a past life regression therapist because I was very interested in knowing my past lives. The session was useless. I saw, heard, and knew nothing. Blank. I was very unhappy about this, and at the time had a very obsessive overactive mind, so I did not let it go. I was at the gym bicycling while my mind was noodling over how I was going to find a better past life regression therapist…maybe Oprah had a recommendation?

Suddenly a loud male voice boomed in my head: **"You have a life. Live it."** I almost jumped out of my seat. It scared me a great deal and I decided maybe I'd better just follow that advice. (I now know it was stern guidance from Archangel Michael.)

So I proceeded with my life which had me go unconscious to the ancestral patterns running through me; and with my personality at the wheel, I made a fine mess within a few years. The mess concluded with the vision of the end of the rope and the choice to move into a new unknown chapter of my life.

Indeed, that choice to take a 90 degree turn into a new uncharted path has been a fascinating discovery and led me to this place where now I know who I am in truth and love.

Does any of this sound familiar? Has your journey echoed my own? The details may be different, but can you relate to the overall design?

Some of the people I have interviewed on Soul Nectar Show, and the clients I have had the privilege to awaken, were awake from birth. They knew they did not belong on Earth. They knew they were from somewhere else, and wanted to go home. They had a clear connection to their soul family and etheric support, and so maintained awareness of who they really were outside of their human bodies. It feels as if these souls were spared the full brunt of Earth amnesia.

But for those of us who were fully asleep in our Earth existence, we might wonder why. Why didn't I know who I was? Why was I cut off from my higher guidance and soul family?

And all of us might have the question: Why has my life been so challenging? Why have I experienced so many obstacles and difficulties since I arrived here? Why was I placed in the family I was?

The answer goes back to the reason you came. You volunteered to help Earth ascend into a higher consciousness that is being ushered in with the Age of Aquarius. In order for humanity to ascend, there are many ancestral patterns in the human DNA that require karmic cleansing.

One of the reasons Earth has been so stuck in lower vibrational patterns of human behavior is because the very DNA the soul's essence inhabits comes laden with repeating ancestral patterns that are very difficult to resist. Beyond the embodiment of these challenging ancestral patterns is the environmental immersion in a family that has members who have given up resisting the patterns; parents who have succumbed to the expression of ancestral patterns reinforce the patterns in the developing sponge of the child's mind.

Ancestral patterns can be like a gravitational pull that thwart the soul's efforts to lead the egoic Self to make new conscious choices, dragging the Self back into the behaviors that feel familiar to the body. I never understood how difficult it was to resist the ancestral pull of the body until I felt the pull of ancestral patterns in my own body. Growing up, I was perplexed as to why the human species continued to make choices to cause each other suffering, rather than enjoy the garden in which they lived and breathed. Why not play and co-create with all that magic surrounding them? Now that I have succumbed to ancestral patterns in my own life experience, I understand completely the elements that make life on Earth so challenging.

So here we will formally establish two terms to identify different aspects of Self: Soul and Personality. The Soul animates the human body from the Divine Spark that is a bubble of light located just under the heart chakra. As soon as the Soul inhabits the human body, the aspect of it dwelling inside the body is subject to the parameters defined by the body's DNA and memory stored in the cells of the body. The moment the Divine Spark is activated, the formation of the Personality begins. The Personality is like a crust formed around the Divine Spark. It simultaneously covers up the Divine Spark and is powered by the Divine Spark.

Think of the body like computer hardware and the Soul like the power to the hardware box; the essence or Divine Spark brings the hardware to life. The operating system running on the hardware is the conditioning from the body's DNA and early childhood domestication; this is the foundation of the egoic Self or Personality. After awakening, the Soul becomes the programmer of the software and hardware, but some tricky viruses have to be removed first and the system rebooted to allow access (in other words, the Personality lets go of control through some kind of trauma).

The Soul's wisdom up until this incarnation is a key factor in whether or not the Soul will be able to 'crack the code' of the hardware and software to remove viruses and regain programming control. This is why mature souls from across the galaxy have been invited to participate in the Second Wave: more experienced with cracking the code, so to speak, of the egoic Personality Self. (Some part of you probably smiles at this statement because deep down, you've always known this to be true about yourself.)

Never a truer statement was made than by Michelangelo who said that he was not carving the statue of David, but rather, removing all the stone that covered up the statue that was already underneath. In much the same way, the Personality crust covers up the truest self, the Divine Spark, with its DNA-infused perceptual filters.

A crack in the crust is a gift for accessing the Divine Spark. And in the collective consciousness that has been humanity, those cracked Personalities have been called shamans, visionaries, mystics, or in Western culture: crazy.

The thicker the crust, the more third-dimensionally anchored a person is. People with thick crust would never pick up this book. So if you're reading this book, you can relax about your crust.

Which leads me to describe another common attribute of Second Wave people: a serious interest in self-help. People in the Second Wave can be obsessed with figuring themselves out, healing themselves, helping family members, and pursuing careers that involve helping others such as psychology and healing arts.

That inner impulse was planted in you by design.

We talked about how humanity needs its DNA to be healed of karma and ancestral patterns in order for the collective consciousness to ascend in the Age of Aquarius. The Second Wave volunteers are here to help with that process by healing their own DNA of karmic and ancestral patterns. In so doing, we heal seven generations forward and seven back.

To heal something, you must experience it personally. You can't heal other people's stuff. Not really. Even as a healer, we are only holding space for the person to heal themselves. However, there is a bonus to healing ancestral DNA. The ancestors seven generations back who are beyond the veil are receiving the healing gratefully because they see clearly from their crustless Divine Spark that this is a gift. Their consent to this healing actually ripples backward through time and uplifts the whole timeline and ancestry which then ripples forward through time on its own. The ancestors seven generations forward starts with your own children for whom you have authority to heal up until their age of separation from you as a parent, which is around 18 years old. And there's a little backdoor you can use via recapitulation to heal your children back in time and correct situations you now see had a negative effect. Of course, all of this comes with the utmost respect for the individual souls and their chosen life journeys which might include the suffering they are experiencing.

With your upgraded DNA and vibrational resonance, you positively impact anyone who shares your DNA by placing the upgrade at the edge of their field as a 5th dimensional invitation for them to accept this part of the healing puzzle. The closer the DNA match, the more powerful the upgrade.

All you do is show up with your upgraded resonance and everything else happens at the 5th dimension naturally. Those who share your DNA will choose for themselves whether or not to receive the upgrade. They have free will, so they can say no. However, many will gladly receive the upgrade as it creates ease and grace in their lives.

So is the grand plan starting to make sense?

You came here into a specific ancestral line that embodied certain lower vibrational human patterns so you could heal them within yourself and ripple that healing forward and back to thousands of humans. You also came here to experience generalized patterns of human suffering so you could be a vessel for healing that pattern for humanity overall.

Some of you came in to embody, experience, heal and then vibrate out healing energies like beacons of light. Some of you came in to do that plus aid in the healing of others. And some of you came in to hold the truth of who you are, so that you could wake up your sleepy friends in the Second Wave and get us activated.

In the book "The Three Waves of Volunteers and the New Earth," Dolores Cannon states *"Many of the first and second wave do not want to have children. They unconsciously realize that children create karma, and they don't want to have anything tie them here. They just want to do their job and get out of here. Many of the do not marry, unless they are lucky enough to find another of their own kind."*

My channeled insights indicate that this is not exactly true of the Second Wave volunteers. A segment of the Second Wave volunteers are here to heal ancestral DNA and to birth children of the Second and Third Waves on Earth. Otherwise, how would we ensure these souls get off to a good start in the world? We are the soft landing that allows them to surpass us.

No matter what you've experienced since you were born in this lifetime on Earth, it all had a purpose that serves the Second Wave. Do you know your purpose? If you didn't already know your purpose, is your purpose beginning to be clear for you now?

The invitation is to shift your identification from the Personality you always thought you were, to the Divine Spark under all that crust that knows why he came here, why she came here.

I hear this message from the Great Spirit: "You have had your human experience. Now it's time to close that book and move forward. We have other agreements to attend to."

♥

Suggestions

Your Healing Journey *Spend a few minutes journaling about your family history from this new vantage point of healing ancestral DNA and patterns of human suffering. What have you healed in your own life experience that you inherited from your ancestry?*

Remembering Yourself *Repeat this mantra daily from Paul Selig's channeled works, and begin listening to the Audible versions of his books starting from "I Am The Word." What do you feel as you say the mantras? What do you notice about your knowing after a week or a month?*

> *I know who I am in truth and love*
> *I know what I am in truth and love*
> *I know how I serve in truth and love*
> *I am here, I am here, I am here*
> *I am free, I am free, I am free*
> *Word I Am Word with this intention*
> *Word I Am Word*

Your Divine Spark *As you tune into your Divine Spark with the accompanying meditation (available at www.thesecondwave.media), can you feel your Divine Spark as separate from your Personality? Journal about your observations.*

Quotes

"Owning our story can be hard but not nearly as difficult as spending our lives running from it. Embracing our vulnerabilities is risky but not nearly as dangerous as giving up on love and belonging and joy—the experiences that make us the most vulnerable. Only when we are brave enough to explore the darkness will we discover the infinite power of our light." — Brenè Brown[4]

"He was a Starseed. He wanted to escape, but the stars brought him here. Now he is homesick " — Pankaj Kumar

"We are not humans having a spiritual experience. We are spiritual beings having a human experience." — Pierre Teilhard de Chardin

"Less than one half of 1% of this planet has to make these choices for a fully changed planet to occur." — Kryon

"Behind the scenes, heroic battles wage the likes of which have never been seen on this planet before yet go completely unnoticed by the people who will ultimately benefit from them the most." — Scott Mowry

"We are a fractal of the big picture; we accelerate the Global Shift with inner transformation." — Sandra Walter

"The path of the Initiate is to reach upward for the highest potential, regardless of what may or may not be happening around him or her." — Hathors channeled by Tom Kenyon

There is a jewel Lotus flower unfolding, deep within my soul.
To be a jewel Lotus flower unfolding is the highest goal.
om mani padme hum, om mani padme hum, om mani padme hum
♥

Closing the Book of Fate, Opening the Book of Destiny

The more you wake up to yourself as a member of the Second Wave, the more your energy field and life will vibrate so as to pull you towards your purpose. It will become more and more clear which aspects of your life stay behind in the Book of Fate, and which parts transform to aid you in your purpose work in the Book of Destiny.

These transitions of people out of your life will likely trigger inner conflicts because of agreements you thought you had to keep that came from your human conditioning. It can be strange to feel like it's totally fine that your parent is no longer actively part of your life because your domestication might have been to call and visit your parent to be a good son or daughter. You might worry that you are doing something wrong by not visiting, and might feel perplexed that your parent is also making no effort to be a part of your life. Relationship based in obligation is not authentic, and as we move out of codependency towards interdependency, these relationships will feel forced and contrived and will falter.

You are not required to keep the Welcome mat at the door and open the packages of psychic hate mail that people send you who are operating in a denser vibration. You must protect your inner knowing as it blossoms with appropriate loving boundaries that honor yourself and allow others to do as they will with their life experience. You are not responsible for assisting people mired in hateful thinking to 'come to the light' simply because you have, or formerly had, a relationship to them. The best gift is a respectful self-loving boundary with neutrality about their potential life outcomes. Do not take it upon yourself to be responsible for the soul evolution of your parents, adult children, spouse or former spouse, or friends. Let each soul be the determiner of his or her fate. There will be other incarnation opportunities for every soul to make the journey to the Upper Room that Paul Selig references in his channeled work.

It's literally as if the old movie continues to play exactly as it always did with all the same players, except you are not in the cast. You've moved over to the next theatre where you're in a fascinating sci-fi movie with all new super powered friends. Their movie does not have a role for 'galactic visitor' or for someone who sees right through the plot and can predict the ending. That's called a spoiler. Also, the gig is up. You're not really part of their cosmic play. You're a temporary participant. You're probably not going to stay on Earth for a bunch more karmically-entwined lifetimes. So if you do visit their movie, don't expect them to understand your movie and new perspectives.

Another reason people drift away from you is because as your energy and vibration ascend, some people with thicker crust will feel irritated by your presence. It won't feel good for them to be around you anymore. This is a misunderstanding on their part that is likely difficult to explain to them. The reason they feel uncomfortable is because higher vibrational energy actually shakes loose the crust around a person's Divine Spark. When the crust is shook loose, it can be like an inner cloud of noxious energy; for lack of a better analogy, an inner fart. That is very unpleasant as I'm sure you've experienced. But as the noxious energy (perhaps its fear, anger, grief, and so on) expands and rises, it eventually dissipates and leaves you feeling freer and more at peace. People who overly identify with their crust will not be very willing to experience this inner noxious cloud, and therefore will avoid you thinking there's something wrong with you, or that 'you' make them feel bad.

And then there are the entities. The easiest way for me to describe how this works is to go to the physical example in the body of parasites. If you eat foods high in sugar, gluten, alcohol, and so forth, you cultivate a gut where little parasitic creatures like to make their homes. They feast off your body and they send signals to your brain to tell you to eat more of that stuff they prefer. The only way to get rid of them is to start eating healthy raw vegetables and improve the gut environment to the level where healthy bacteria can survive and thrive, weeding out the unhealthy parasites.

At the etheric level, there are entities that feast off the auric field that surrounds the human body. These entities eat anger, fear, grief, regret, shame, guilt, and all other heavy human emotions. It's in their best interest to provoke situations where the human host will respond by generating these 'foods.' If the entities perceive you as a threat to their meal, they will create situations to either have their human host provoke argument with you, or they will send thoughts to the human host to get them to avoid you. Most crusty humans think this is nonsense, and so the situation persists even though their life may be filled up with examples of the truth of these statements. If you are feeling unsettled by this information, it is something to further explore within yourself to verify its accuracy.

As with any imbalanced gut biome, the Earth has become a breeding ground of entities who, rather than clean up the internal environment like helpful scavengers, actually 'farm humans' for lower vibration emotional energies. What we are doing now is putting the system back into balance by removing a large segment of the entity population and recycling the energy. Many humans have had a parasite attached to their energy field since they were children, making it hard for them to become aware that the aspect of self that gets angry/resentful/hateful/depressed is not actually part of their essential nature; at least to the degree it has been occurring in their inner climates. Humans include the entity in their sense of identity, and until the entity is removed, it's hard to grasp the extent to which the entity has injected false information into their consciousness.

Focus your energy and resources on aligning yourself as closely as you can in your energetic field to your own true vibration. You simply must cleanse your auric field and raise your vibration so you can make the inner transition from egoic-led living to soul-led living. You must cultivate the inner awareness to know what thoughts and decisions are coming from the egoic Personality self, and which are inspired from your soul. Many times the things our soul calls us to do are not 'comfortable' and familiar and do not 'make sense' to our Personality self; remember that any parasitic energies are not going to prefer your energy ascending, and will generate confusion and doubt to block your progress. We must gain commandment of the Personality self and take the actions inspired by our souls to truly be in service to the Great Spirit. Allow the things to fall away that are not in resonance with your soul without resisting the transition. If grief arises, use your tools to process the emotional experience and support yourself in whatever way you need to let go. You are the protector of your Inner Child and Divine Spark; call on your etheric allies to help you.

Part of the transition into the Book of Destiny is to choose healthy boundaries, release your history as aspects come to your attention, and choose over and over again your Destiny path. Following the practices in 'Clearing Your Channel' later in this book, doing Shielding meditations to grow the strength of your inner light, and extricating yourself from human paradigms of suffering (such as the Triangle of Disempowerment) are all ways to claim your Destiny path. Especially be sure to sleep in a protected clear space so that your consciousness can roam freely during the vulnerable hours you are unconscious. As you pull away from the Book of Fate, the forces that want to keep you mired in the old patterns of your history will tug harder at you. You'll become more aware of these forces as you disentangle yourself and raise up your energy. Then the forces start resorting to attacks while you sleep because you're in a vulnerable state. I experience a psychic attack like a big, loud white noise in my ears that feels menacing. It usually enters into my dream in a way that seems innocuous which leaves me unprepared for it to leap out and expand with fear energy in an effort to provoke me into a fear reaction. In the past, the energy used to prevent me from speaking out against it in my dream because the first place attacked will be the throat chakra which has the power of your Word. I recommend opening sacred space and inviting support while you sleep, as well as using sage to clear your bed and pillow before lying down for the night. Black tourmaline or other black stone under your pillow is also helpful. Cover up any television screens with cloths so as to prevent a portal through which entities can enter your space while you are vulnerable. Play Solfreggio frequencies in your bedroom every day to cleanse the field. Notice what difference these remedies makes in the quality of sleep you are able to receive. Run an experiment and implement these ideas for a week or a month, and notice what happens. Be your own scientist.

As you ascend your energy and move more deeply into the Book of Destiny, you will experience fewer and fewer psychic attacks. I only notice them now when I have done something to lower my energetic vibration, such as having a glass of wine. On those evenings that I know my energetic vibration is lower, I am very mindful to cleanse my auric field thoroughly, cleanse my bedroom, remove psychic cords and attachments to people who may be projecting hateful energy, and employ my allies to protect me as I sleep.

Moving forward, it is vital that you make connections with other Second Wave volunteers to form community for support and boosting of your energetic resonance to form a new collective consciousness field that can start to penetrate and vibrate through the overall collective consciousness of Earth with the frequency of truth and love. Be very mindful in this work to access higher states of consciousness when forming collective ideas so as to prevent the construction of Personality-driven initiatives. You can participate in group meditation to tune into Source for inspiration, leaving any personal agendas at the door; clear your mind, and be open to receive without attachment to the outcome. Notice the alignment in messages received from members of the group meditation; what is the common thread? In this way we collectively move through the smoky mirror to something more clear and true for the planet.

As a member of the Second Wave, I fully understand how painful it can be to make this transition and let go of those who you used to define as family or loved ones. I know how the Inner Child feels to witness new information about one's parents that challenges the innocent interpretations of youth, and to make the journey to accept yourself as your own Inner Parent. I know the sense of responsibility and guilt that needs to be relinquished and replaced with faith and trust that your former people have everything they need to make the next part of their journey without you. Letting go of this aspect of yourself is a necessary part of fully accepting your true identity. It's as if holding onto your former life is a roadblock that keeps triggering your mind into old ways of thinking, and creates doubt about the messages that start arising from your true identity. But if you are in the identity that considers those people to be your family or your friends then you're still allowing the Personality to cloud your consciousness and this can create a push-pull dynamic to your progress that delays your growth.

Rather than grieve the ones who choose not to come, be grateful for the presence of those who choose to make the journey. Trust your process of evolution and give yourself the spaciousness to undergo the necessary metamorphosis. It's very possible that once you are squarely centered in your true self, you can engage your human family from an entirely different identification that allows you to hold tremendous love and compassion for their pathways through life while remaining true to yourself. Give this possibility the space it needs to unfold in the perfect way for you.

♥

Suggestions

Ritual to Release Your Book of Fate Rituals are a powerful way to operate at the mythic level of consciousness which is the language of the soul. You can think of the mythic as the place of storytelling, artwork, opera, and so forth. One ritual I love is the Three Card Story which I learned about with the Four Winds Light Body School. The simple version of it is to get a deck of Tarot cards with pictures you like. Then hold the deck as you shuffle the cards and ask the Great Spirit to reveal to you three cards that represent your life journey: past, present moment, and potential future. Then pull the three cards. You can now write your own epic story, tapping into the mythic part of your brain, to translate the images you see on the card and the significance they bear for understanding your life journey. Once you have written your story, you can choose to release it with the element of fire which is a powerful force for transmutation. You can create whatever ritual you desire to release your Book of Fate.

Imagine Your Book of Destiny! Meditate about your destiny and drop into all the potential timelines that stretch before you. I offer a guided meditation for my clients and students that helps them to visualize their destiny lines and select the highest destiny. Once you have a 'feel' for your highest destiny line, receive messages and inspiration to help guide you. You can also create a vision board with pictures you pull from magazines that resonate with the same feelings and messages you received during your meditation. Key: you're not selecting images from your mind, but from your heart and soul knowing. You don't have to understand why certain images need to be on the vision board. Surrender and allow yourself to discover how everything on the vision board is perfect.

Quotes

"Although the two terms are often used interchangeably, there's a marked difference between fate (which is known as karma among Eastern traditions) and destiny (also known as dharma). Fate is a course that's been predetermined by our family, our history, our genes, and our emotional wounds - it is the prearranged and seemingly inevitable series of events that happen to us. [...] Destiny, on the other hand, is the purpose and calling of a life, and it can be discovered and realized. Early Greeks believed that fate was spun from a certain thread, and that once it was woven into a cloth it was irreversible; they saw destiny, on the other hand, as a force or agency that could intervene to reweave the cloth of fate."
— Alberto Villolo

"Sometimes the road of life takes an unexpected turn and one has no choice but to follow it to end up in the place one is supposed to be."— Khusbu Shaw

"Until you make the unconscious conscious, it will direct your life and you will call it fate."— Carl Jung

"It is in your moments of decision that your destiny is shaped."—Tony Robbins

"It is not in the stars to hold our destiny but in ourselves."—William Shakespeare

"What if...everything you are going through is preparing you for what you asked for?"—Derin Cag

Walking the Beauty Way

The Beauty Way is an indigenous path of the heart and personal power in right relationship to all of nature. Walking the Beauty Way requires a great deal of humility, listening deeply, and being in service to all of Earth's creatures. The Great Spirit invites us to step onto the Beauty Way and bring ourselves into right relationship with the Earth. As we step onto the Beauty Way, we tap into the greater consciousness of the Earth and lead our lives from harmony rather than discord.

Stepping onto the path requires an initiation and act of courage. And every new gift of power is preceded by a new initiation. "To whom much is gifted, much is expected" is the creed. You demonstrate responsibility and right relationship with the gifts you're given, and you're invited to keep Walking the Beauty Way. As the path unfolds, you discover your essential self and bring your divine light more fully into your Earthly form, and this is where the rubber meets the road for manifestation and serving your purpose.

As you Walk the Beauty Way, you glimpse behind the curtain to understand more of life and its underpinnings. You become aware of the consciousness of all forms of life—from stones to plants, mountains, trees, animals, birds, elements, and the Four Directions. Life becomes easier as you realize you can ask for help of these allies at any time. You call for help, these allies come immediately. And in reciprocity, when the allies call for your help, you offer it freely in gratitude and service.

Did you know that the tree in your front lawn is connected to all other trees across the globe via a massive connective web under the surface of the Earth? You can be just as connected as the trees when you Walk the Beauty Way, and thereby know with a vastly greater wisdom than is possible to achieve by using your brain to gain knowledge.

The longer you Walk the Beauty Way, the more the Great Spirit reveals to you about life, yourself, loved ones, nature, power, and co-creation. You learn to interface directly with the Divine Consciousness that created all that is, and that consciousness becomes your teacher in every single moment of your life. You learn to wield your power for the good of all and become an instrument of the Divine in action on the Earth.

To Walk the Beauty Way effectively, it's helpful to have the guidance of lineages that have walked The Way for thousands of years on the Earth (especially if you are new to Earth). This grounded wisdom is invaluable for your journey. Many of you probably have felt a pull to nature and Earth-based spirituality your whole life, but may have been swayed against it by religious doctrine. Heed your natural inclination towards Earth-based spirituality. You might even be in a body that has a Native American or indigenous lineage; having the DNA makes it easier to access the wisdom from your ancestry for Walking the Beauty Way, and so many of you chose to be born into families with this DNA ancestry.

In my own journey, I have Cherokee ancestry from my maternal lineage. It took a bit of spiritual work, but I was able to be reconnected beyond the veil to these ancestors and even received Walk In assistance from a Cherokee Chief that helps me to this day. More about Walk In guides later in the book. My Cherokee ancestors led me by synchronicity to indigenous people who practice a path of fire like the Cherokee: the Q'ero shamans in the Andes mountains of Peru. I was also led to the Toltec from Mexico who also practice a path of fire, and now connect with the Huichol as a primary lineage. I am immensely grateful for the indigenous people who protected their wisdom for Walking the Beauty Way through a great deal of threat and suffering, and then turned around to share it today with people from the very cultures responsible for their torture. That is incredible grace, humility and service.

Because of many wise indigenous people from the Q'ero, Huichol and Shipibo, I have awakened and begun Walking the Beauty Way to experience great love, joy, prosperity and purpose. Within my own vessel, I am fulfilling the prophesy of the Eagle and the Condor.

From the Pachamama Alliance:

> *The Eagle and the Condor is an ancient prophecy of the Amazon that speaks of human societies splitting into two paths - that of the Eagle, and that of the Condor. The path of the Condor is the path of heart, of intuition, and of the feminine. The path of the Eagle is the path of the mind, of the industrial, and of the masculine.*
>
> *The Eagle and the Condor prophecy of the Amazon speaks of human societies splitting into two paths - that of the Eagle, and that of the Condor. The path of the Condor is the path of heart, of intuition, and of the feminine. The path of the Eagle is the path of the mind, of the industrial, and of the masculine.*
>
> *The Eagle and Condor prophecy says that the 1490s would begin a 500 year period during which the Eagle people would become so powerful that they would virtually drive the Condor people out of existence. This can be seen in the conquering of the Americas and the killing and oppressing of the indigenous peoples in the subsequent 500 years - up to and including today.*
>
> *The prophecy says that during the next 500-year period, beginning in 1990, the potential would arise for the Eagle and the Condor to come together, to fly in the same sky, and to create a new level of consciousness for humanity. The prophecy only speaks of the potential, so it's up to us to activate this potential and ensure that a new consciousness is allowed to arise.*

I have been told by the Great Spirit that part of my function is to bring Earth-based spirituality from Condor lineages into the Eagle world. I am red on the inside, meaning I am native, I am indigenous, I am path of the heart. And I am a Caucasian woman on the outside, meaning I look like the people who are driven by the consciousness of the Eagle. I am a bridge between worlds. And this also fulfills the prophesy of the Warriors of the Rainbow.

Here is a part of the story as told by Cherokee woman, Lelanie Anderson.

There was an old lady, from the "Cree" tribe, named "Eyes of Fire", who prophesied that one day, because of the white mans' or Yo-ne-gis' greed, there would come a time, when the fish would die in the streams, the birds would fall from the air, the waters would be blackened, and the trees would no longer be, mankind as we would know it would all but cease to exist.

There would come a time when the "keepers of the legend, stories, culture rituals, and myths, and all the Ancient Tribal Customs" would be needed to restore us to health. They would be mankind's key to survival, they were the "Warriors of the Rainbow." There would come a day of awakening when all the peoples of all the tribes would form a New World of Justice, Peace, Freedom and recognition of the Great Spirit.

The "Warriors of the Rainbow" would spread these messages and teach all peoples of the Earth or "Elohi." They would teach them how to live the "Way of the Great Spirit." They would tell them of how the world today has turned away from the Great Spirit and that is why our Earth is "Sick."

The "Warriors of the Rainbow" would show the peoples that this "Ancient Being" (the Great Spirit), is full of love and understanding, and teach them how to make the "Earth or Elohi" beautiful again. These Warriors would give the people principles or rules to follow to make their path right with the world. These principles would be those of the Ancient Tribes. The Warriors of the Rainbow would teach the people of the ancient practices of Unity, Love and Understanding. They would teach of Harmony among people in all four corners of the Earth.

I have come here to be a Warrior of Rainbow light, and perhaps you have as well? I remember being on journey in Peru with the Q'ero. We had just finished an expedition to Ausangatay, the Holy Mountain, and I had journeyed all the way to the Rainbow Lagoon which is at 16,500 feet. It was a challenging trek, but I prayed for help from Ausangatay; I was able to make it up the elevation and steep climb. The next day we were in ceremony with the Q'ero shamans and they said something about me I did not understand. My friend translated "They think you are the Rainbow Keeper."

Ever since that day, I began channeling Rainbow Light in healing sessions for my clients, and became aware that I was able to bring people etherically to the Rainbow Lagoon and Ausangatay for healing and work with their guides on drum journeys. The clients and students who work with me also receive energetic and etheric support from the Q'ero, Huichol and Cherokee lineages, as well as the Shipibo lineage that I study with for an understanding of plant power. Everything you cultivate within your vessel as a fulfillment of these prophesies becomes a gift for anyone in your sphere of influence. Although these lineages have lifted me up, I also understand it's my job to keep evolving myself and forging my own pathway for my family, clients and students.

Are you drawn towards Earth-based spirituality? Do you love Rainbow light? You may be one of my Warriors of the Rainbow sisters and brothers.

♥

Why Earth-Based Spirituality Is A Powerful Uniting Path

I sat in the church at the funeral for my husband's friend, and I was resonating with the messages being conveyed by the pastor. Until he said "I am your connection to God." No. Wrong. Each human is a physical manifestation of a multidimensional spiritual being that is connected directly to the oneness we call 'God.' There is no intermediary necessary between a person and the Great Spirit. In fact, having an intermediary is what distorts a person's spiritual connection. The belief that a person needs someone outside of themselves to connect them to what they already are is preposterous. And the outright guidance by religious institutions and texts to ignore your own intuition as somehow prone to 'evil' has disempowered people from accessing their own direct connection to the Great Spirit. Quite simply, whether you are a 'guru' or a pastor, you are in egoic attachment to your self-importance whenever you convey any message that a person needs you to access 'God.'

A large part of the suffering of human kind is arguing over whose interpretation and path to 'God' is 'right.' This is like the flowers arguing with the deer over who has more right to be on the planet. It's ridiculous. And it's dangerous. Dangerous because humans have something called free will which means they can directly disobey guidance from the oneness of the Great Spirit and create separation. Dangerous because of religious systems that instruct people they are forbidden to know their own truth, and must rely on and be loyal to the political structure of a church, else be cast out. We have all of human history to see the result of thinking one path to the Great Spirit is better than another. We've bred generations of people who are terrified to go direct to God...as if the Great Spirit would ever allow anything to interfere with the sincere desire of a person to know their own truth in love.

From the time I was a child I was amazed at how people placed so much faith in any book that was written thousands of years before, after being handed down through oral tradition. One simple game of Telephone between just 5 people exposes the truth that there is no way that any of those ancient texts have the absolute truth direct from the mouth of God. And even if those texts managed somehow to capture with 100% accuracy the information being downloaded in 30 AD, the allegories were written to appeal to the intellectual capabilities and common experience of people at that time.

In a world where someone might club you to death for stealing a loaf of bread, is it any wonder that a human being speaking of love would be revered? And in a world where people's consciousness was struggling at basic survival, thick in the reptilian brain, unable to access higher reasoning, is it any wonder that they would think someone like Jesus to be otherworldly? What do you think would happen if a lightworker of today was teleported back in time to 30AD?

The victim-rescuer paradigm has gotten deep roots in modern culture from Jesus, and I'm quite certain that was not intended by Jesus. Forgiveness is a gift you give yourself on Sunday because you know you are going to change your ways as a result of your new understanding. Forgiveness is a gift you give yourself on Sundays because your heart has been opened seeing how your words and actions impacted another person, and the integrity within yourself is strengthened to learn from your mistakes and be a better person from this moment forward. But when you think you've got a back-door pass to do whatever you want, and all you have to do is call on Jesus before you die to forgive it all, doesn't that open a door to being a less responsible human?

Whether or not you believe in karma, it is real. The truth is karma. What you do unto others is done unto you. You get to experience the action and the reaction. The more karma you create in a lifetime thinking you have a back-door pass out of it, the more karma you get to rectify in the next lifetime, and the next, and the next; until you finally figure out that you've been sold a bill of goods about being rescued from yourself. Jesus was never here to save you. He was here to teach you that you can save yourself.

I thank my mother for gifting me a blank slate for my spirituality to naturally flourish. Because I was not programmed by religious doctrine, I have the gift of seeing things for what they are. I also have the gift of no fear. I'm not afraid of speaking out loud these things because they're true, and I'm not risking being outcast from my spiritual home by speaking them. If it provokes anger in those who read it, then I suggest that anger is there for a reason. Any place we feel triggered is a perfect place to explore deeper, to listen to ourselves and find out why. What's the underlying structure or belief that is causing the anger within you? When you invite the help of Jesus to understand your anger, what do you learn?

The reason I say that Earth-based spirituality has the potential to be a powerful uniting force for humanity is because of some obvious things. First, we all live on the Earth and should definitely understand her. She's the larger conscious body within the Great

Spirit that birthed you. You are made of Earth and you live and breathe in her aura. Just like you have an auric field that surrounds your body, the Earth has an auric field surrounding hers that we call atmosphere. We live inside her aura.

Second, the escalation of disease and mental illness on the planet that coincides with the rise of 'indoor people' is stunning evidence that shutting yourself away from nature is detrimental to your health and your psychology. You don't need to read the scientific article proving that a person who spends 15 minutes in the woods has improved mental health. All you need is to run the experiment for yourself to confirm what you already know is true. Having to prove obvious things like this is a great example of the egoic control within our collective Western consciousness.

Third, if we are the keepers of the Garden of Eden, which is Earth, then shouldn't we understand the needs of the plants, animals, elements, minerals and so forth that we are here to tend? The belief that humans have a higher level of divinity than other lifeforms on Earth is also born of ego. When you have sat in plant ceremony and opened your mind to the consciousness of any one of nature's teachers, you will see that you have a lot to learn indeed from these gentle wise beings. Humans are the savages trying to claw their way up in evolution. We are the grand experiment of the galaxy. The indigenous shamans with whom I've studied know that the plants, rocks and animals have a lot to teach us, and they listen and learn with great humility.

Fourth, indigenous cultures have not forgotten their ancestors. Beyond the veil are your ancestors, ready to assist you in your life. The ancestors are in a higher dimensional plane and can see things you cannot see from your Earth-bound perspective. The ancestors know life on Earth, and have sage advice to give you from the vantage point they now enjoy. I once had a Lakota teacher connected to work with me solely because of the encouragement of his ancestors. When you connect with your ancestors beyond the veil, you can save yourself a lot of trouble and egoic resistance by consulting with them.

Lastly, when you convert your mentality to Walk the Beauty Way, you realize that you are responsible for your footprint on Earth. You start to open to your senses to perceive the Great Spirit, rather than reading about mankind's interpretation of God in a book which is a very smoky mirror. When you start using your senses and experiencing the Great Spirit through all that you see before you, a whole new understanding of yourself emerges. You align yourself to the heartbeat of the Earth, you come into harmony with life, and you become aware that all disharmony in your life has been caused by your ego and the egoic collective consciousness on the planet. (Side note: Another factor causing disharmony are entities and parasitic beings which have been created by humanity's collective agreement.)

One of my earliest memories was a commercial on television that was part of a national campaign to pick up trash. It featured a Native American with a tear rolling down his face. When you live close to the Earth, and are in harmony with it, you know when you are consuming too much. You know when you are out of balance with the life around you. You know it's wrong to litter, to pillage the resources, and to build, build, build way beyond our needs. You know it's wrong to cut down forests, and dump waste into rivers and streams. And you definitely know it's wrong to wage war on another people by killing thousands of buffalo out of spite.

Notice how Western culture is primarily geared towards creating indoors people. This way, the ego can keep doing what it's doing to destroy the Earth, and lie to itself. The more unhealthy the humans are, the worse food choices they make, the more distracted they are with drugs and alcohol, the greater their detachment from their own bodies through the 'miracle' of pharmaceuticals—the longer the ego maintains control and keeps itself out of harmony with the Earth. All of these behaviors promote the lingering of lower consciousness, density, a sense of powerlessness to change anything, and drama that perpetuates more karma.

Consider quantum physics for a moment. The particle is the 'thing' which is the material form, and this is the domain of the egoic self. The wave is the Great Spirit which is the energy, the void, and the spaces between the things. If you look at life today, you see humans incredibly overwhelmed by a lot of doings and thinking and things. Thing-thing-thing-thing-thing…leaves no 'space' for the Great Spirit.

Watch within yourself all the excuses your mind creates, and then generates 'proof' of in your external environment, so you can avoid doing what you know at a soul level you are here to do. When you find yourself saying you don't have time/money/resource/ability to do something right now that you know at a soul level you are meant to do, adopt an attitude of "Oh, is that so?"[5] Don't believe it. Do what your soul is telling you to do. Claim your spaciousness and invite your divinity into your human experience by Walking the Beauty Way.

When you Walk the Beauty Way, you rediscover your personal power as a sovereign being. You realign to your true self and regain your mojo. You gain the energy to make decisions that leave things better than you found them, not worse. You experience expansive time. You stay in harmony with the Earth, unleash the crust from your heart so you can feel, and tune into higher wisdom for your next steps. Your direct connection to the Great Spirit yields the perfect wisdom in the moment for your path. To open your channel to higher guidance, it's helpful to change habits that block higher consciousness and maintain a daily spiritual practice of clearing your energy body.

Walking the Beauty Way can seamlessly integrate with Christ Consciousness, which is direct interfacing with the ascended masters who teach and share a pure frequency that upgrades you energetically to the level of consciousness that you can go direct. Not only go direct, but more fully embody as your multidimensional self in your human form, which is exactly what Jesus was demonstrating all those thousands of years ago.

The 'second coming' is you, choosing to take responsibility of your life and learn how to walk the Earth consciously. For these teachings, I recommend the series of texts channeled through Paul Selig beginning with "I Am Word."

From a space of being in your own knowing, you can integrate a church environment in right relationship to your sovereignty; you have a direct connection to the Great Spirit, and you evaluate the information being shared from that place of knowing to discern how true it is for you.

Until you take responsibility for your own life and choices, and choose to grow spiritually as a sovereign co-creator on the Earth, you will remain stuck in the cycles of karma created by the victim/perpetrator/rescuer paradigm. How many more lifetimes do you want on Earth? You can have as many as you require to advance your consciousness to the next level.

♥

Tap Into the Wisdom of the Earth

You may have come far across the galaxy and be an old soul of thousands of lifetimes on other planets, but you are now on Earth. The Earth is a unique consciousness that offers many wise teachers in the form of stones, plants, elements, mountains, animals, birds, aquatic beings, insects, and most of all, the Four Directions, Earth, Moon, Sun and stars.

The ancient wisdom traditions of Earth know that all of life is a teacher in this dimension. I first began a dawning awareness of this truth when studying with The Four Winds Light Body School which teaches students to cultivate a mesa, or medicine bundle, filled with stone 'people.' This is a tradition from the Q'ero shamans in the Andes mountains of Peru. High up in the mountains there are not a lot of other kinds of life forms, but there are plenty of stones! So the Q'ero tradition focuses on gaining wisdom from the kuyas, medicine stones, on their sacred mountains. The stones are not inanimate. They are operating in a dense structure, but they are animated and can do a number of amazing things. Some kuyas seem to pop right out of your mesa and disappear when it's time to move on...it's pretty magical (and disturbing to people with control issues).

When stones become kuyas in a mesa, they serve to hold a vibratory frequency of healing that uniquely serves your particular path, and all those you are meant to assist. They are capable of holding multidimensional information from clients about the matter that needs healing simply through breath (blowing it into the stone), and also tracking the location of that virus or code within the client so that it can be released through the healing session.

The kuyas are also capable of transmitting advice to you as you hold them in your hands and meditate; you simply come to a new awareness in the stillness as you work with your kuyas. They don't 'talk' or form words like humans do, yet they communicate exactly what you need to know through your feelings that bubble up into thoughts within your mind as a result of the feeling sense.

A very interesting experiment I ran when I was a student at The Four Winds was to go into a crystal shop and wander around until a stone grabbed my attention as being a potential kuya. I let my heart lead the way. Without knowing anything more than that the kuya had attracted my attention, I then referenced a book about stones and discovered how exactly perfect this stone's gifts were for my current life work that would be addressed in the next class. In this way, I learned to trust that the stones were communicating with me.

Now I am constantly amazed during healing sessions at how people will pick a kuya from my mesa for a healing, and that particular kuya holds a 'hook' from my own training that the client is currently wrestling with on their own journey. In this way, the kuyas offer healing from their natural gifts to my clients, as well as give me very useful information for the healing session about what I should be tracking in the client.

Whether or not you cultivate a formal mesa, it is very helpful to work with stone allies to improve your boundaries, grounding, self-compassion, discipline, prosperity, calmness, confidence, and so much more. I encourage you to run my experiment! Walk through a crystal shop and see which ones 'speak' to you, then look them up to see their gifts. Do they directly address your current life challenges?

Meditate with them, put them in your pocket, or place them on your desk or by your bed.

Mountains, or apus, have mountain spirits in the spiritual understanding of the Q'ero people, and indeed, I have found that the apus can be very powerful allies. Ausangatay is the holy mountain of the Q'ero in Peru, and Quemado is the holy mountain of the Huichol people in Mexico, and I work with both of these ancient teachers on my own journey because I study in these lineages. You can always call on the big apus around the world to assist you—such as the Mt. Kilimanjaro in the Himalayas or Mt. Shasta in Washington—but what's most powerful is growing a relationship with an apu for whom you have personal significance. Is there a mountain near you that you love to visit? Start talking to the mountain in your prayers and invite support.

Elements—earth, fire, water and air—are amazing allies on your journey. I've personally worked a lot with fire because the indigenous lineages with which I study are a path of fire. Fire is purifying, empowering, and transforming. When I lead firewalks, it's about so much more than facing your fear of walking barefoot across 1300 degree coals. Walking across fire is an ancient tradition that helps people to cleanse themselves of dense energies and blocks, and fill up the tank with beautiful light. Sometimes people receive a fire kiss when they walk across the fire, but when they consult a foot reflexology chart, they see truth in where the fire was trying to go within their bodies to give them support.

I learned this particular lesson when leading my first two firewalks. On both occasions, I got a blister in exactly the same spot! Upon looking at my foot reflexology chart, I saw that the location was the solar plexus, which is the seat of personal power. The organ was kidney in Chinese medicine. It made sense to me; I was making a huge leap in my business by stepping into the responsibility of leading other people across 1300 degree coals...I needed some confidence and will power to hold this new larger responsibility!

Of course, I tested the theory by going to a naturopath and telling her nothing of my fire kiss. I answered all of her questions which she used to determine what part of me needed support. The result: kidneys. The fire had already told me this!! So I laughed out loud in glee and revealed to her that fire had already told me that I needed kidney support and showed her my foot. She was amazed. Since then, many of my firewalking students have run similar experiments with truthful results that demonstrated the fire was working with them for healing in their bodies, emotions, minds and spirit.

The work of Masuro Emoto proves the power of the element of water as an ally. Water captures and holds any intention we desire. Why not fill up a pitcher of water and bless it with the intention of prosperity love and joy, and then drink from that water all week? And when you consider that our bodies are made up of at least 60% water, doesn't it make sense why it's so important to speak kind words about yourself?

The Earth herself is a powerful ally for your spiritual journey. You can stand barefoot on the Earth and receive calmness within 15 minutes. There are plenty of studies out there that explain how this works, but the best way is to go out and try it for yourself. I also love lying on the ground belly to belly with the Earth…that works even better to clear your mind and energetic clutter.

You can also perform earth painting to resolve a current life challenge. In this process, you use earth elements to construct a healing circle for yourself, and then within the circle you recreate the feeling sense of your challenge with earth objects such as stones, leaves, sticks, and so forth. Seeing and feeling your challenge represented this way often leads to aha moments of understanding which then allow you to move things around in the healing circle to invite new possibilities. I learned this process while studying at the Four Winds Society Light Body School, and use it regularly in my spiritual practice as well as teach it to my students and clients. It can also be called a sand painting.

Plants are also incredibly potent allies. Flower essences are a good introduction to plant power as they have the ability to help you overcome a range of challenges simply by placing a drop on your tongue whenever you think of them. The power of flowers was discovered by Dr. Edward Bach who began experimenting with the ancient practice of collecting drops of dew from flowers in the early morning hours, and listening to the flowers about what gifts they could offer. Now many people experiment with creating flower remedies or elixirs. The best way to discover flowers is by running your own personal experiments, like I suggested with the stones.

Over the last few years as my spiritual journey brought me to the jungle, I have learned about the powerful plant teachers on Earth. I began by embodying the plant teacher Ayahuasca, and quickly learned that she knows everything about me; she can see into every dark cranny and is extremely no bullshit about pointing it out. Beyond being in a ceremony, the plant teacher lives in your body once you've welcomed it by consuming it. If you quiet your mind and tune into the wisdom of the teacher, you can hear it every single day. In other words, you can work with the spirit of a plant, and the resonance of a plant you've consumed that's in your cellular memory, without taking the plant into your body. I often invite Ayahuasca into my healing sessions with clients who have never consumed her medicine, and yet they receive healing from her and have related to me that they felt her. You don't need to keep a container of Ayahuasca in your fridge and drink her every day to be enlightened. You simply need to tune into her wisdom and listen for her guidance.

There's been a lot of sensationalism about Ayahuasca, and so I'll just speak to the fact that this teacher is only meant for those who truly desire to ascend your consciousness. It's not for recreation or visuals or a psychedelic experience…it's to gain wisdom about yourself and the Universe, and to heal. Let's not disrespect her the way we have marijuana or tobacco.

On the subject of tobacco, this teacher is powerful and wise when you are in right relationship with him. This teacher has been worked with for thousands of years by indigenous people. Tobacco is for cleansing your energy field, rooting out darkness, and blowing prayers to the Great Spirit. This teacher is not for inhaling for a superficial high or addiction; if you use tobacco in this way, there are physical consequences.

I started working with tobacco as a result of studying with the Shipibo people who use mapacho to cleanse auras, heal hearts, and blow prayers. I began by mimicking what I saw, and asking for the support of tobacco in my healing sessions and for my personal prayers. The mapacho often tasted very bitter and strong to me, and I didn't really like it, but I knew instinctively that it was a powerful healer for me to build a relationship with.

Then I went to the jungle and consumed tobacco as part of a dieta with a Shipibo shaman. The moment I began working in an embodied way with the tobacco, it no longer tasted bad to put my lips to a mapacho cigarette, or to blow the smoke during healing sessions and prayers. It had no foreign taste at all in fact. And when blowing it, it just felt like blowing air. It no longer smelled bad. It became a part of me. Tobacco started tuning into my thoughts and body sensations, and I could ask for its help with every inner wobble. I would feel a self-doubt and psychically communicate with the tobacco in my body "that right there tobacco…help me with that!", and I could feel the weakness resolved and the holes plugged up instantly within me.

Now I consider tobacco to be a very good friend and ally, and I have a tremendous amount of respect and humility when working with him. I am incredibly grateful that tobacco shares his medicine with me every single day.

I've had the experience of a Shipibo shaman introducing my energy field to many different plant teachers while I was in Ayahuasca ceremony. I felt each plant consciousness penetrate the membrane of my auric field, and *glub glub glub* down through it, revealing to me a landscape of visuals and feelings from its consciousness. I'm fairly certain that what each plant showed me was their home planet where they came from to be here on Earth as a galactic emissary; each plant consciousness experience felt like a whole different world. I felt quite queasy during this process, but I knew this was because the plants have a much higher level of frequency than my human body, and they were helping to raise the frequency of my body by upgrading my cells with their wisdom.

So many people think of plants as inanimate things that grow on Earth; but truly, they hold incredible wisdom and ascended consciousness that only the most humble of us humans will ever discover. So if you're intentions are not of the highest regard, you will likely find it very frustrating and fruitless to pursue plant medicine work such as I am describing. This wisdom is only given to those whose intention is to use it for the good of all. And since we are human and dealing with lots of lower vibration impulses, you can expect some discomfort when working with these teachers because the consciousness held within your cellular structure needs to be upgraded to effectively interact with the plants. Sometimes the only way to really upgrade is to physically purge out of your body the lower vibratory patterns. If you want to work with plants, you've got to be ready to puke.

Please be mindful if you are interested in plant medicine work to choose a shaman with high integrity and humility. We are all in process, but some shamans are a lot further down the path. Use discernment. People on the plant medicine path are likely to shine you on a bit when you ask about ceremony because they don't want to jeopardize their safe growth container; so be patient as you prove yourself to be a worthy companion for this journey. Responsible humans on the plant medicine path have a good grounding in taking personal responsibility, sitting through discomfort, and not creating drama. It's very helpful to start with the energetics (energy healing, working with stones, and so forth) and garnering spiritual discipline with regular practices and awareness, before starting down the plant medicine path.

Now let's talk about animal allies. Steven D. Farmer has done amazing work writing about all the animal allies on the planet that are here to work with you on your journey. For the purpose of this discussion, animal allies can also include birds, dolphins, butterflies, and so forth. You can have personal animal allies for your lifetime, to help you through a specific challenge, or as part of a lineage with which you study. For example, the Q'ero have legends about Hummingbird, and even built Machu Picchu in the shape of a Hummingbird. Many South American lineages work with jaguar and condor and serpent. North American lineages often work with wolf and buffalo. The Huichol people revere the deer which they call Kayumari. When you begin working with an indigenous lineage, their animal guides will begin showing up in your life to help you Walk the Beauty Way.

Right before I began studying with the Four Winds, I had a mystical vision of a hummingbird rising up in rainbow light. This vision spontaneously happened at the end of a drum journey where I was visualizing living in the home I wanted to buy. As the hummingbird hung in rainbow light, and I experienced a state of awe, I stopped drumming and the phone rang. Upon answering it, I learned that the owners wanted to receive an offer from me for the house I desired. Just ten minutes earlier, the owners had been in contract with another buyer!

As I opened to the magic of hummingbird, I soon realized that this was an animal spirit guide for my life. I changed my name on social media, began surrounding myself with totems of hummingbird, and drew a beautiful artwork from the vision of rainbow light which still hangs above my altar today.

My relationship with hummingbird has been incredible awe-inspiring and powerful. She has lifted me out of the darkness and back into joy and the knowing that anything is possible. To help me realize the deep love of the Great Spirit, hummingbird periodically manifests almost unbelievable mystical moments. In one such moment, I was on a solo retreat in the woods for three days with nothing but a tent and a jug of lime water. At the end of the first day, I found a big rock to stand upon as if it was a stage, and I began singing into the woods a healing song I was learning as part of my training with the PowerPath. I was calling in support from the plants and animals and Four Directions when I suddenly had an inner giggle and I called for the support of hummingbird. Before I could finish singing the stanza, a hummingbird swooped in from across the forest and hovered eight inches from my third eye. It stayed there for a good minute or more...it felt like an eternity of wonder. Then I acknowledged that hummingbird came when I called, and it nodded and flew away.

When you call on your animal spirit guides, they always come when you call. They may not manifest materially in front of you, but rest assured, they are there for you. You can feel them if you quiet your mind and listen.

Which leads me to the Four Directions. Like many Westerners, I thought the south, west, north and east were just there to help me navigate a map to get somewhere. In a way, they are. But they are so much more than that. The Four Directions are beings of light (some say they are the Archangels) that surround the Earthly plane of existence. When I started studying with the PowerPath, I received a whole new profound understanding of the Four Directions, even though I had been inviting them into my world in sacred space for years prior. It was like a magic door opened when I heard my teachers opening sacred space, and felt their relationship with the South, West, North and East. "Whoa! These are not just words," I realized. "These are beings of light that are listening to me. I can build a relationship with the Four Directions!"

In many ways, this knowledge feels most sacred to me, even as it is the first teaching I often give students. It's the gift that keeps on giving. As each layer of understanding peels back, you become in deeper love and wisdom and connection with the conscious framework of planet Earth. It's astounding. You cannot manipulate the Four Directions. You can, however, bare your open heart and invite them to guide you on your journey.

I teach my students about the Four Directions in the best way I know how: resonance. When you hear the resonance of opening sacred space from someone who has cultivated a respectful loving relationship with the Four Directions, you tap into a doorway within yourself through which you can begin Walking the Beauty Way. I highly recommend beginning each day by opening sacred space and inviting the winds of the south, west, north and east to guide you. There is an invocation for opening sacred space that you can practice along with an audio that is a companion to this book. Practice, practice, practice every day. At first it may feel foreign, but soon the doorway within opens and you begin a most amazing journey guided by the Four Directions.

♥

Your Personal Conversation with the Divine

By Walking the Beauty Way, listening in a new way through nature, and experiencing spirituality through your senses and knowing, you begin to have a personal conversation with the Divine. You are a unique being and what you require to advance you on your soul journey is like no one else. Learn how to tune within so that you can have a personal conversation with the Great Spirit: what's right for others may not be right for you. Cultivate a personal relationship with the Great Spirit, and learn to trust the guidance you receive, because Earth's understanding of the Great Spirit is quite murky from thousands of years of human-based manipulation of spirituality for control and power. Some of the messages conveyed through religious institutions withstand the test of truth, and others…not so much.

A basic measurement for discernment is whether the message is based in fear, judgement, lack, control, shame or blame. These messages are part of the murky understanding of a world whose foundation has been suffering, and these lower-vibration messages serve to create more suffering.

Messages that resonate as truth within your being and call you towards greater self-master and integrity are worthy of consideration; pass these messages through your own truth filter as you converse with the Great Spirit directly.

Yet another reason to have a personal conversation with the Great Spirit is because not everyone is aware at the same level. Some people are only aware of the third dimension. Others are aware of the fifth dimension. Others are aware of many more dimensions beyond the fifth. At each layer of reality, you can become aware of new information, new life on the planet, and new refinements to your spiritual code of ethics. The more refined your awareness, the more you perceive nuances that escape the attention of those operating in lower vibration and density.

This is part of the reason why our awakening souls are being placed in mental hospitals in the West. Western civilization is largely disconnected from a personal exploration of the Great Spirit, and has closed down the senses and intuition required to perceive non-visible aspects of reality in other dimensions. Especially the aspect of the Western world that has been placed in responsibility for psychology. The focus on mental processing (and arrogant disdain of spirituality) has led to a disconnect with intuition, feeling senses, and psychic capabilities. Simultaneously, the Western world has been opened to greater spiritual awareness through yoga, breathing techniques, somatic healing, and a plethora of technologies to raise consciousness. The stagnant understandings of Western psychology paradigms do not know how to handle spiritual awakening; thus there are record numbers of credentialed psychologists leaving behind formal methodologies in favor of spiritual training. They want to actually help people, not lock them up.

As an awakening empath, it's best to be selective about where you share your personal experiences as you raise your consciousness. Sharing about entities, for example, does not work well with a psychiatrist or in a mental hospital. They are operating in the paradigm of the mind; they have no grasp of other dimensions or spiritual realities. Get yourself a mentor who has successfully integrated and grounded her spiritual awakening to learn tools and practices for navigating yours with ease and grace.

When you realize that there are 8 billion realities on Earth, and 8 billion conversations with the Great Spirit operating simultaneously, you can make the bridge towards respecting and honoring each soul's spiritual path. You can also make the bridge to not take it personally when others around you have no idea what you're talking about if you share spiritual insights from a higher understanding. Do not diminish the insights given to you by the Great Spirit simply because others around you operating in lower vibration have not yet ascended to the point of receiving a similar insight. Likewise, do not indulge in arrogance about your spiritual understanding; everyone is on the path and moving at his or her own pace. This is not a race. It is a journey that requires volunteers of the Second Wave to have patience, understanding, discernment and compassion.

Making these bridges of understanding within yourself serves your role as an emissary of the Second Wave. We are here to bridge to a world where each soul can freely explore his or her own spiritual communion with the Great Spirit, and we can collectively enjoy the diversity of conversations that the Great Spirit can simultaneously hold with each of us, while synchronistically connecting us at pivotal moments for the good of all. Isn't that incredible? Let's leave behind judgement and be in awe.

♥

Opening Sacred Space

Stand facing the South
I welcome you Winds of the South. Help me to be connected and grounded with the Earth, feeling her beneath my feet and knowing I am safe and held. Help me to be in presence, and to feel you all around me in a way that my mind cannot deny. Help me to feel your love and support throughout my day so I know I am beloved.

Stand facing the West
I welcome you Winds of the West. Help me to see into my shadow to identify those aspects of myself that no longer serve me so I can make a new choice. Help me to have wisdom and discernment for what should go and what to grow. Help me to let go with ease and grace of what does not serve, and expand into a higher destiny.

Stand facing the North
I welcome you Winds of the North. Help me to receive the gifts of my ancestors, and to release ancestral karma that no longer serves my highest destiny. Help me to know who I am in truth and love and to stand in my power with an open heart. I welcome my guides, ancestors and angels to help me throughout my day, and give permission for nudges to redirect me onto a better path.

Stand facing East
I welcome you Winds of the East. Help me to open to a new possibility today, beyond my wildest imagination, that leads me to the highest destiny available to me at this time. Help me to fly high above my life like Eagle and get that bigger perspective so I can understand my life at this moment and be in peace.

Touch the Earth
I welcome you Mother Earth. Thank you for this beautiful body that is healthy and strong. Thank you for all the allies you sent to help me on my journey including the mountains, rivers, stones, plants, animals, birds, and trees. I welcome the wisdom and guidance of all of these allies throughout my day.

Raise Up to the Sky
I welcome you Father Sky, Sun, Moon, and Star Nations. Thank you for filling me with beautiful sunlight, moonlight, starlight and rainbow light. Thank you for light codes to help me ascend my vibration towards my highest destiny.

And thank you Great Spirit, you who is known by a thousand names and yet is unnamed-able. Thank you for bringing us all together. Thank you for allowing us to sing this song of life. Aho!

Quotes

"A truly indigenous person is one who has intimate connection with Mother Earth and who embraces all human beings in order to get along with them. There is a respect for diversity, which is part of the circle of life. Pluralism is valued, so it does not matter what color you are, for there is no being better than or less than, no negative judgement. We are all connected. Indigenous peoples listen to not only their minds but most importantly to their hearts and to what Mother Earth is saying."
— Anita Sanchez from The Four Sacred Gifts: Indigenous Wisdom for Modern Times

"All the suffering and drama in your life is the result of what you have learned. Whatever you learn is alive. The image that you have of yourself is alive, and it lives in your mind. That image is not you, but it will use everything it perceives to justify its own existence. It is not you, but it is eating you alive and destroying your happiness." — Don Miguel Ruiz[6]

"Although your mind resists it, the fact is that you have a choice between having the life you want or having the reasons you can't have that life. You can have joy and peace, or you can have that big black bag full of all the sorrowful incidents and accidents that happened to you in your childhood or in your last relationship. You can have your wounds or you can have your glory. You can live the life of a victim, burdened by the traumas of your past, or you can live the life of a hero, but you can't do both. If you want to feel empowered, you need to make a conscious decision to dream a sacred dream and practice courage."
— Alberto Villoldo, PhD[7]

Does this Sound Familiar?

We can learn so much through the mirror of someone else's experience. This phenomenon points to the deeper truth that we are sharing in a collective experience that reflects itself through many different lenses. In other words, what's happening at the macro level is happening in many different variations at the micro level. So as I share highlights from my personal story in this section, can you find yourself in it?

ભ

Ever since I can remember I've felt like a novice, constantly learning from other people that surrounded me (and this went on way after childhood, actually most of my life). They seemed to be in on the games people played with one another. They seemed to innately understand the rules of the human dynamic. I always felt this innocence within me that was curious about why people behaved the way they did. I found myself watching others as if I was absorbing information that would someday make sense to me. And I felt like I didn't really have the same grounding in the human dynamic that they had, like I had joined a party that had been going on for hours so I was missing a lot of information, and I had to act as if I had been there the whole time even though I'd only just arrived. People were a total mystery to me, and they felt treacherous, like they could turn on a dime and be nasty.

At the same time as I quickly learned to be cautious with people, I also had this ability to see the best in people. I could see the highest potential of a person as an overlay to their personality that somewhat obscured the more shadowy aspects of their current demeanor. This soul vision made it difficult to see the truth of the moment for the person and what they were hiding from me, or what I was unable to clearly see. In my dating life, my rose colored glasses proved to initiate many lessons in adjusting my vision from soul to person.

Of course, the people around me picked up on my lack of savvy, and often created situations to hook my gullible nature so they could have a laugh about my naivety or take advantage of me. I found myself drawn in by people who seemed cool or aloof or exclusive in some way. What I didn't realize at the time is that these people were good at hiding things about themselves, and my attraction to them was driven by an innate sense that not everything was at it seemed on the surface. Exercising my psychic muscles to penetrate the façade taught me a great deal about human nature and the machinations of the egoic self which now serves me well in my purpose work.

I often felt confused why people would go directly against themselves to lie, cheat, steal, bully, and so forth. Didn't they have an inner bolt of lightning that told them a behavior was wrong (I now call this 'out of right relationship')? Why would they ignore that? I felt it pretty clearly, and I could not understand why others seemed to not get it when something they were doing was out of integrity. I remember many times being shocked to find out that someone had been lying to my face or talking behind my back; I had seen the goodness in them rather than their current state of being and the lessons they were choosing to learn. Even the slightest transgression I did would provoke deep reactions within me that I would obsess over how to resolve for days or weeks. Why did other people seem impervious to this inner struggle?

As a result of my innocence and my attraction to people who were experts on human manipulation, I found myself in four decades of mental sparring where I intimately learned about gaslighting, projection, narcissism, energy vampires, and mental/emotional abuse (without knowing those terms until much later). My emotions and senses would convey information to me that produced knowings which, upon sharing with the person, would be denied and projected back onto me with blame causing me to experience confusion and self-doubt and a sense that it was "all my fault." The feeling that it was all my fault would be confirmed and reinforced by the people in my life creating a shame spiral where I felt like I could do nothing right, and questioned the purpose of being here in this life if, as people were telling me, all I did was create trouble for them. And then I became hooked into the negative spiral and engaged in poor choices as a retaliation, and felt myself going against my nature.

Since we live in a duality on Earth, the opposite was also true, which compounded my confusion. I was often put up on a pedestal and told that I was talented and smart and a shining star that could do anything she set her mind to. I was given the idea that I was somehow special and different than others since I could easily pick up new concepts, ideas and skills and implement them. I was told my voice was like an angel when I sang. People said they loved my energy. I seemed to be able to do things very quickly that challenged others, and excelled at doing things I'd never done before. My light, capacity for intense joy, and generous nature pulled people in to me when I was lit up and feeling good. People loved me when I was feeling good and bringing them along my happy ride. But it seemed there was no room for me to be anything other than happy if I wanted people to stay liking me. If I was feeling sad or angry, the heaviness or intensity of my emotion seemed to repel people and make them avoid me.

Somewhere along the line I noticed that people seemed to be leaning on me, or draining my energy, or requiring me to lift them up. I felt a great deal of responsibility for the state of their human condition, as if I was able to do something about it but was neglecting my duty. I felt like a big elephant in a tiny china closet, and there wasn't room for me to freely express myself for fear of causing a negative reaction in others around me. In fact, there was an odd feeling of being privileged and hugely gifted, and needing to compensate for it by doing my part to help. I felt guilty for my gifts, and like I was supposed to be of service to those around me and help them; even as a child I felt this way. Aren't children supposed to be taken care of, and not the other way around? Much of this was perceived and felt rather than overtly discussed.

It seemed to me that the game on Earth was fitting in. However, there was no way I was going to fit in on Earth. No matter what I did, I stuck out like a sore thumb. I knew from early in my life that I wasn't like other kids, and life reinforced this message with a series of relocations where I lost friends and climbed the mountain to make new ones with each new town. Every time we moved and I went to a new school, I would watch the dynamics. I got good at spotting who the kids had chosen (whether consciously or not) to pick on; these were the kids who instantly offered their friendship to me. At the time, I saw them as the rejects that the other kids had decided were not cool; now I wonder if they were just like me…Misfits on Earth. Probably the latter; their open hearts and genuine natures gave them away in retrospect.

Throughout my life I found myself retreating to my safe space and to nature. I loved being in my room alone with my imagination, and had ample opportunity to do so as a latch-key child. I now believe that this situation of being a latch-key child was Spirit's way of keeping me separate from other kids with a healthy buffer so I would not be overly influenced by their ideas and conditioning. Although I loved having other children over to play, I was just as happy when they all went home.

I've always needed a great deal of alone time to be creative, to be quiet, and to connect with that which is bigger than me…the expansiveness beyond the physical that was easy to experience in nature, or when creating something from inspiration (such as writing or painting). My preference has always been to commune with nature or to be doing something inspired from my higher self. I have always loved being with the trees, mountains, rivers, rocks, and other creatures in nature. To me, the Great Spirit is present in nature with a level of clarity that is hard to access in human realms which are distorted and polluted by the chattering mind, egoic self, free will, and the madness of the collective consciousness. I totally resonated with author philosophers like Henry David Thoreau who I felt were kindred spirits.

But I didn't come here to dwell on the mountain top, and I knew it. I came here to be of service to humanity. I actually remember the moment that I knew it was time to dive back in to humanity; it was a distinct realization that my time on the mountain, roaming around for hours in nature and being a hermit, needed to be balanced with human interaction. I needed to return to the village and start understanding those human beings and their psychology. It actually felt like a non-negotiable assignment I knew I had to undertake.

As I began my assignment and entered the human classroom, I dove head-first into mind mazes and thought tunnels and emotional fireworks that led me to psychotherapists for two decades to deal with increasingly dramatic life experiences. I was learning about human psychology from the inside out. The challenges in my life brought me lessons to help me to understand myself and my inner workings, and eventually to reveal to myself who I really am so I could step forward in my soul capacity on Earth. When I got the message I was to write my first memoir, *Awakening To Me: One Woman's Journey To Self Love*, I heard distinctly: "You are going to write this book as you heal to chart the course out of madness. Be absolutely transparent and vulnerable." I reluctantly, but pure-heartedly, did as instructed.

During the two years writing my first book, and for five years after, I experienced a gradual awakening to my true self. There were little visions and signs every step along the way that could easily be missed or dismissed through unconsciousness and doubt. Luckily, I kept stepping deeper into the journey and Walking the Beauty Way.

For now, I'd like to share some things in the following sections that I've learned that might apply to you as well.

♥

Being Empathic Is A Super Power!

The message I hear from the Great Spirit is that there are several components of human design that volunteers in the Second Wave have chosen to embody, and these are the components I have been experiencing in this incarnation so that I could assist the Second Wave volunteers. You are invited to look up your Human Design chart[8] so you can see whether your human design aligns to these qualities. The primary quality we share in common is being emotionally centered and empathic.

The reason Second Wave people are emotionally centered is because feelings provide vastly complex information that gets underneath the conscious mind and down deep into the subconscious where the landscape of energies reside that we are healing. With feelings, you see past words to the truth by stretching your feelers into the subconscious terrain of another person. In fact, you likely have the ability to shapeshift into another person and feel what they feel: their emotions, body sensations, and so forth. Shapeshifting as I have experienced it is an energetic process of slipping into another person's energy field while remaining present in my own body. Then my body and feelings start mimicking the other person's as I'm working with them for a healing session.

I have had this psychic gift throughout my life. I knew when someone was upset even if they acted like they were happy. I could feel it. I knew when someone was talking about me behind my back. I could feel it. When I tuned in and looked past my rose-colored glasses, I knew when someone was lying. I couldn't prove it, but I could feel it. There were a few close relationships in my life where the person flat out denied my knowing, and it really disturbed my trust in my feelings. With all the years of practice using my psychic gifts in my training and business, I now see that my insights were accurate. It's just that when you've got access to a person's entire subconscious through your feelings, you see much more than they do about themselves. They may not be ready to know what you know, and reject the information out of self-protection. Some clients have told me it took years to process and understand the insights I gave them during healing sessions. One client spent 3 years with a psychotherapist to process the insights. That blew me away! Three years? But that's the difference with a Second Wave volunteer. Your soul vision is very clear once you activate it in your human body.

To really use this gift, you've got to have an empty emotional bucket. This means that you must allow your feelings to flow as they arise until they dissipate and pass. If you judge or repress your emotions to fit into the conditioning of the systems around you, you clog up your primary superpower. It's interesting that our world shames emotions and instructs us to stuff 'negative' emotions and not express them because this path disempowers the emotionally centered individual from their primary psychic gift.

Second Wave souls born with a beautiful capacity to feel are often born into a family that is operating at life's surface with a lot of crust covering over the heart due to conditioning that runs through the ancestry. These emotionally capable individuals make their families uncomfortable with their perceptiveness and responsiveness, and are led to believe there's something wrong with refined emotional perception and emotional depth. Empaths are brought to the psychiatrist to 'fix' their powerful range of feelings, and further disempowered by prescription medications designed to create a glass wall between them and their feelings; otherwise stated, between them and their psychic gifts. Meanwhile, under the glass wall, emotions are still brewing and stepping all over them creates inner discord that leads to disease in the body. And if the empath is encouraged to stuff their emotions rather than explore them, they may not come to the realization that a lot of what they're feeling is actually repressed emotional energy from the people who surround them. In other words, empathic people often unconsciously take responsibility for, and process, the repressed emotional energy of other people because they mistakenly think the emotions belong to them.

To make emotional perception your super power, you've got to learn how your emotions work so you're comfortable with them. When you're comfortable with emotions, people around you can relax about it too. When you explore your emotions, you'll get to know the difference between your stuff and others' stuff. As you allow yourself to feel the full range of your emotions, your inner resiliency increases as well as your capacity to hold space for others.

Part of making your emotional perception powerful is becoming crystal clear about boundaries with others. Without clear boundaries, you lose yourself in others as you tap into their fields and shapeshift into them. Prevent this confusion by knowing your own frequency, shielding your auric field, and staying grounded and present as you tap in. You also need clear agreements about what you will mulch or process for others, and what is actually their responsibility. Without clear agreements you can pick up 'negative' energy from other people and feel burdened. Over the next nine years we are supported astrologically in extricating ourselves from co-dependency structures and opening to interdependency. Boundaries and knowing yourself are critical to this transformation.

You also need to let go of the "too much" story. When you do, you'll expand into the tremendous blessing you bring with your emotional centered human design. Your capacity to feel everything is a huge gift that you bring to help wake up sleeping humans who have suppressed their feelings and disconnected from their hearts. Only unfeeling people can do the unthinkable things that happen in today's world. What's more crazy? The person who feels everything and weeps at the state of our world? Or the person who is numb and carries on business as usual?

♥

It's Normal To Need Personal Space

A lot of Second Wave volunteers are also 2/4 Hermit-Opportunist in human design type. This explains the preference to spend time alone rejuvenating and connecting with oneself. This profile helps you with your mission by giving you a predilection to be alone along with a desire to get out there and make stuff happen at appropriate times. Part of the function we have in the Second Wave is to transform our own suffering to ascend our vibration, to boost that ascended vibration through rest and rejuvenation, and then to radiate that ascended vibration out into the world to raise the vibration of the collective human consciousness on the planet. Another part of our function is to mingle out in the human population, thereby touching etheric bubbles with other humans and spreading our ascension codes like wildfire.

Do you ever wonder why you get the download you need to go to a specific place, but you don't know why? By visiting certain sacred sites and vortexes, like Machu Picchu in Peru or Mt. Shasta, your energy field is replenished and uplifted as you pick up helpful ascension vibrations that are then embodied in your cellular memory. You collect energy signatures by visiting the places you're instructed to go. Then you can bring these collected vibrations back to your family or community for automatic upgrade of everyone who meets you. You'll also get inspired to go to public spaces, like restaurants or theatre, and that could be so you can uplift the people in that space with your auric field upgrades.

Do you ever wonder why you need so much time alone? It's partly because you need spaciousness to saturate in your own vibration without interference from others' signals so you can deeply tune into your own station. Sleeping in your own space without other humans within a 10 foot radius is very restorative for this purpose. When you reduce the static and can more clearly hear your own higher guidance, your whole energy field can relax which allows it to replenish itself and integrate whatever upgrades have been acquired by your healing work and travel.

When you venture back out into humanity with your restored energy field, people may say things like "I don't know why but it feels great to be around you." This is why. Many people on Earth cannot muster the energy to push past their conditioning and hurdles to move their bodies to a place like Machu Picchu or to do the intense energetic cleansing work we are doing. It's easier for you as a Second Wave volunteer to move in the world and accomplish these tasks because you are in the world, but not of the world. You are not as burdened by thick karma as many souls that have spent lifetimes in Earth school. Either you have completed most of your studies on Earth, which means your soul is lighter and ready to transcend this plane of existence. Or you are not from Earth and are only stopping in for a lifetime to assist in the transformation of the planet. Have you ever wondered why it seems so hard for most people to get the simplest things done, while over in your life you've had to deal with four times the load? Hopefully it makes more sense now.

Have compassion for your fellows now that you have this bit of insight.

Another role of the Second Wave is to cross-pollenate the planet by migrating through different human communities to share energy signatures and ideas. Think of our role as that of bees, creating the honey from the pollen of many various flowers spread out across the countryside. In school, did you make friends with the smart kids, the sports kids, the rebels, and so forth...kids that typically didn't like each other? As you visit various groups of people, you become aware of energy signatures and patterns of consciousness that would be served by a new understanding and frequency. This might present itself as feeling negative energy which you then seek to heal within yourself. What you are actually doing is integrating this new information into your honey and upgrading the entire system to a new level of understanding and frequency. Your attention gets hooked by the feeling of dissonance, or not compatible with your field, and your instinct is to return your inner system to harmony, thereby creating harmony between the dissonant or incompatible energies you encountered on your personal journey. In this way, you create a healing for humanity on the micro-personal level that can then ripple out through your energetic signature to everyone you encounter on your journey.

Your innate ability to be a chameleon facilitates this cross-pollination by your inquisitive nature and desire to blend into different communities, and by your ability to shapeshift into others for greater energetic/emotional perception and understanding. When you were operating unconsciously, your vessel led you to believe the negative energy you were feeling was a result of something you did and so you were inspired to seek personal development tools and practices to heal it. Now that you're operating at a level of consciousness about this dynamic, you can proactively integrate the energies and cross-pollenate without taking it personally as if it is a problem. It's not a problem. It's part of your purpose.

♥

Lifting Others Up

It's in your language. "I'm always lifting him up," "I feel like she's dragging me down," "He's sucking me dry," "It feels so heavy, it's killing me." The density of Earth and the heaviness of lower-vibration energy and emotion can feel very burdensome to the Second Wave volunteers; particularly those for whom Earth is a relatively new experience. There's a natural dynamic that happens when there is bright light: the darkness disappears or falls back. But it is also true that too much darkness can overburden a light and close in on it to snuff it out. The bigger the darkness, the brighter the light has to be to withstand it and turn the tide toward even more light.

Let's use the word 'happiness' instead of 'light' and 'depression' instead of 'darkness.' If an exuberantly happy person enters a room filled with depressed people, the automatic response of depressed people is to be agitated by the exuberantly happy person and turn away into even more darkness. If a modestly happy empathic person enters a room filled with depressed people, the mood begins to shift and the depressed people are drawn to the light of the happy empathic person. If there are not good boundaries, the empathic person 'takes on' some of the darkness that burdens the depressed people, and the depressed people feel a little lighter while the empathic person feels a bit drained and tired. The depressed people feel better and are grateful for the empathic person helping them to feel better as a result of this energy exchange, and the empathic person is happy to have helped.

In fact, the Second Wave are here to lift up the Earth by bringing light and helping to transform the DNA, thereby ascending the human experience. To do so, you may feel you need to soften your light so as to not blind the people you serve who are in darkness; to be more 'relatable.' You may also feel compassion and generosity that prompts you to 'give' some of your light to others to help lift them from their darkness. The key to being in service in this way is to maintain your own elevated vibration by making time for self-care to keep your light nurtured and replenished. You cannot give from an empty cup.

It is strongly urged that you ground your energy with roots into the Earth to stabilize your field and draw energy up from the Earth. It is advised that you discover your own frequency and learn to shield your energy field and plug up the holes for greater vitality and power. It is recommended that you learn to cleanse your chakras and meridians to release blockages and denser energies and promote a healthy vital flow of clean energy through your system. It is helpful to surround yourself in a protective sacred geometry field, such as an octahedron, that allows you to maintain your higher vibratory field with less interference and resistance from your surroundings. You may ask for support from your guides to help you determine the best solutions for protecting and cleansing your energy body.

You are also encouraged to filter your light rather than diminish it. In other words, keep your light bright, and simply add a filter over your light when entering a space where people are more accustomed to darkness to make it more comfortable for them to receive your presence. A bright light is easier to sustain because it is the truth; the dimming of your light is the lie that takes energy to produce.

Although lifting others is part of our agreement in service to the planet's ascension, there is a limit to what you can give. Where the energy exchange gets challenging for the empathic person is when you take on too much burdensome energy from others without replenishing your energy field. In a close relationship, if your partner keeps generating dense emotional energy (repressed or expressed) and does not learn how to lighten the energy themselves, you will 'burn yourself out' trying to lift up your partner. When your partner has a leaky container that can't hold the light, the darkness keeps creeping back in, and he or she keeps drowning and reaching for a life raft. As an empathic person, you may experience 'energy vampires' that deplete your resources and leave you feeling exhausted, yet feeling responsible to keep 'lifting.'

Now is a good time to mention the old adage that it's far better to teach a man to fish, than to fish for him. Empathic members of the Second Wave are encouraged to have very good boundaries around rescuing others energetically. Be the example of good psychic and emotional hygiene, and teach those around you how to care for themselves. When you feel people tapping into you for energetic support, remind them to 'be like a tree' and send their own roots deep into the Earth for energy and stabilization. Teaching your partner and children how to ground into the Earth, and to avoid cording to other human beings, will help prevent your energy from being drained by people in search of light.

In terms of human design type, the message I hear from the Great Spirit is that the Second Wave is primarily comprised of Generators and Manifestor/Generators. This is because we are designed to radiate out healed patterns with our light as we move about the world. We are designed to 'shine our light' and thereby heal the world with the ascended vibrations we have acquired within ourselves through our spiritual practice. We are designed to lift others up with the power of our light.

To accomplish the mission, we must also learn to protect and nurture our light and share it responsibly so we can keep on truckin'.

♥

Belonging and Not Belonging

The normal way that souls incarnate to Earth school is with an entity which splinters into 1000 souls that experience lifetimes on Earth. As each soul evolves individually, the entity evolves collectively. Eventually, the 1000 souls reintegrate back into the entity with evolved consciousness and progress to the next part of the collective evolution of consciousness. After the cycles of reincarnation and reintegration, the entity moves out of the Astral plane of existence and into a Causal plane of existence which is a level of pure consciousness. This information was channeled from an entity called Michael over four decades ago. To learn more, see *The Michael*

Handbook: A Channeled System for Self Understanding by Jose Stevens and Simon Warwick-Smith.

As an entity comes to Earth and its 1000+ souls begin the cycles of reincarnation in Earth School, they tend to experience lifetimes together in rotating configurations. In other words, they reincarnate together into lifetimes to learn the lessons they require for the evolution of their consciousness. They make soul agreements with each other outside of these lifetimes as to what will transpire during the lifetime to help them attain their educational goals. For example, soul A is the parent of soul B in one lifetime, and the next lifetime they trade places. Each lifetime is a curriculum for the soul that advances its consciousness.

Each soul might experience hundreds of lifetimes on Earth before its entity reintegrates.

If you are a mature soul, your entity might be in the final lifetimes of reintegration. In this case, it's likely you are one of the older souls who agreed to be part of The Second Wave to assist with the planetary ascension at this time.

If you are a galactic volunteer, it works a bit differently. What I hear from the Great Spirit is that you are a mature soul, elder soul, or ascended master who agreed to incarnate on Earth for a lifetime (or several) to guide the souls in Earth School towards the ascended consciousness available for Earth at this time astrologically. Probably you feel like you are the furthest thing from a wise old soul because the curriculum you chose for your Earth experience led you to a great deal of humility. This is intentional. With great power comes great responsibility, and you cannot lead others if you don't understand them. In fact, we are guiding others which is to say that we are demonstrating by example, speaking their language, and encouraging them in the path towards highest good. Each soul on Earth is sovereign, and so must choose the higher way of his or her free will.

As a galactic volunteer incarnating to Earth, you also made soul agreements with Earth-bound souls to integrate into their frameworks and help to lift the lineages and teach lessons through embodiment and relationship. To fully immerse in the experience, Earth amnesia was required of you. It is a great service to the planet. Especially as the human aspect of your consciousness often felt a sense of not belonging, and of being in relationship dynamics that were flipped upside down.

The feeling of belonging, but not belonging, is directly due to the fact that you do have a soul agreement to belong in certain families and human systems for your own integration into these systems so you can fulfill your mission. However, you are a newbie to the human system with which you are integrating. These other souls have probably had hundreds of lifetimes together, which is why you notice them naturally gravitating towards one another and forming connections; whereas with you, connections may feel a bit more forced. I hear this message from the Great Spirit: "These are not your peers."

You are there to integrate into the human system and lift it through your soul's wisdom and higher energetic resonance of consciousness. This is happening even if you are seeing everything through your human lens and feeling resentful and left out. This is happening even if the collective story of your human system is that you are somehow problematic or disruptive to their group consciousness and they want to blame you or ostracize you. In fact, you are disruptive to their human system, and that is by design. We are disrupting patterns of behavior and programs of consciousness on Earth that have gone on too long and are ready for transformation and evolution.

You are a messenger of light and inherently disrupting darkness, and you are thereby fulfilling your purpose. Up until now, it has felt like a very lonely position to be in because you have been distributed across the planet into various human systems that required upgrades, and so you have been separated by several degrees from your counterparts in the Second Wave. Going forward, you can choose to connect with other Second Wave volunteers and experience a true sense of belonging because these are your peers.

Another aspect of life that has been challenging for Second Wave volunteers is the feeling that key relationships—such as parent/child relationships—have been flipped upside down. Meaning that as a child you held greater inner knowing about love, freedom and life than your parent, and perhaps felt like you were your parent's teacher. This is a slippery slope for the egoic self to consider, and so bring as much humility as you can when you consider the ramifications of this wisdom. There is no soul any better than another. We are all on the path to learn and evolve, and getting exactly the soul alignments and lessons required to advance us to the next level of understanding. The way this information best serves you is to allow yourself to have compassion for your parent who may, in fact, be a much younger soul who has been doing her absolute best to raise you from the place that she currently stands in her consciousness, from the place that he currently stands in his consciousness. And, I hear the message from the Great Spirit that you signed up to be a teacher on Earth at this time through your human systems with which you integrated. So be the demonstration of love that you are capable of being.

You can think of yourself as a rogue soul who joined a very skilled and wise squad of other rogue souls to form a collective soul pod that entered Earth School with the specific mission of elevating the consciousness of the planet from the inside out. It might sound really sexy, but in fact it requires incredible due diligence in practicing self-mastery to carry out this work. Your journey probably also included very radical demonstrations of the patterns of human suffering that you were healing through embodiment, which in itself, is incredibly humbling. You can think of it as a PhD program in navigating egoic human structures through personal embodied experience to bring the light of consciousness.

♥

From Tailspin To Triumph

The tailspin on Earth has been generational cycles of abuse, suffering and judgement. People full of pain tend to inflict pain on others. It's like playing a game of hot potato. The person with the hot potato (pain) wants to toss it over to someone else to hold since it's too hot for them to hold. Wanting to punish or have justice from people full of pain that inflicted pain is adding more pain to a system full of pain, and expecting things to get better. Things don't get better that way. More pain into a system full of pain equals greater pain and an entanglement with the system of pain in your own life.

No matter what pain you experienced during the course of your life from people full of pain inflicting pain onto you, there is one huge triumph over the pain that you can attain in your lifetime: Reclaim your innocence. Despite all the suffering, reclaim your innocence and be victorious.

Innocence can be thought of as childhood play. Have you ever seen young children at play? They co-create the rules of the game on-the-fly, and evolve it from one form into another seamlessly as new inspirations arise. When they are in flow and all implicitly understand the 'new rules', there is a joyful ease you can witness as they evolve the game. Perhaps you remember experiencing this as a child?

As clashing ideas arise in the group, there's some momentary separation and argument which is quickly resolved so long as the allure of the co-creation game is strong. Soon, they are back in agreement and flowing together as they evolve the rules of the game.

When you reclaim your innocence, you co-create your life with the Great Spirit much like children co-create their games. The essential nature of the cosmic dance is much the same as children playing in flow with one another. You lead from inspiration, and then are led from inspiration. Your inspiration delights others who come along, then others' inspiration delights you and you come along.

To play and dance with Great Spirit, you must release your history, and the identity you claimed because of your interpretation of your history. Your history will stop the flow of the game because of your attachment to it. When you are blocked in your manifestations, this is likely the cause. You have momentarily gotten hooked on a branch of your history while the river of the Divine flows all around you. The river never stopped flowing. The cosmic dance continues all around you. It's you who has stopped dancing. You are free to stop dancing. Perhaps you desire to consider something, or think about your past to gain insights, or feel your feelings. You may pause as long as you want.

When you want to continue the cosmic dance, you must realize that you have paused yourself, and unhinge yourself from the historical branch that hooked your attention. Often the unhinging process is about releasing a judgement about yourself or another, or letting go of a story you've told about yourself that is not in alignment with where the Great Spirit desires to lead you. You can look within to discover the specific hook that stopped your flow, or you can trust the Great Spirit and release all of your history in one fell swoop with a powerful decision. I like to call on the Spirit of Death and release all of my history and identity in a meditation that I have recorded for my clients.

After the release, you open with curiosity to discover what the Great Spirit wishes to show you about yourself. Anything from your history or identification that requires your attention will resurface when appropriate. In other words, you can't simply brush away all the soul work you're here to do with your Spirit of Death broom. However, you can save yourself the effort of figuring out every little thing that you need to release to move forward, which is a really handy trick of the ego to keep you stuck in thought tunnels considering things rather than doing the cosmic dance with the Great Spirit.

The more full you are of innocence, the less dense and sticky you feel inside. Keep removing the layers of conditioning and identification born of your history, and unfolding into playful co-creation with the

Great Spirit with a greater and greater sense of faith, trust and wonder. Stop worrying about when you'll be 'there' or 'done.' Take the journey in curiosity of what there is to discover.

♥

Clearing Up Your Channel

For best results, you need to go direct with consciousness so you can be tuned into the information you require to fulfill your mission on Earth. Things will be happening very rapidly, so the Great Spirit prefers that you have a strong clear signal to your station and can reliably tune in without a lot of interference. This facilitates you receiving direct moment-by-moment assistance in your mission.

The time has come for self-honesty with regards to your self-care practices. The time has come for spiritual discipline with self-care practices. You know what you should be doing to create a clear channel for the information to flow to you. But here are some reminders:

- Avoid substances that create interference with your pineal gland and third eye. Your pineal gland connects you to higher spiritual frequencies, so it is important to keep it clear and healthy. Top things to avoid: fluoride (e.g., in tap water, toothpaste, and mouthwash); social drinking of alcohol (more than one glass infrequently); non-ceremonial use of tobacco; red meat; poultry injected with antibiotics; junk food, fast food, and packaged food; disruptive noise in your environment; flashing lights (television and other screens); inner disruption (stress and worry).

- Substances to consume to enhance your pineal gland and third eye functioning: chlorella, spirulina, and wheatgrass remove metal toxin buildup and may reverse pineal gland calcification; foods rich in iodine including spinach, broccoli, seaweed and fish; oregano oil; apple cider vinegar; beets or beet juice. (Reference: *Top Foods for the Pineal Gland*, Global Healing Center) Supplements you can take include Alpha Lipoic Acid (ALA),

Turmeric, 5-HTP, Vitamin D3, and EPA/DHA (Omega 3 oils). Refer to your naturopath or to *Power Up Your Brain* by David Perlmutter, M.D. and Alberto Villoldo for specific doses and frequencies.

- Avoid sugar in your diet because sugar promotes unhealthy bacteria in your gut biome which can distort your intuition since the gut mind is a big part of your knowing. Promote better knowing with healthy bacteria in your gut by eating lots of vegetables, fruits, and live cultures of healthy bacteria such as kombucha.

- Clearing your chakras to remove blockages and energetic 'crust.' You can use a rattle to disturb the energy within your chakra and then use your fingers to swirl your chakra energy counter-clockwise and flush out debris. Alberto Villoldo describes this technique in the book *Shaman, Healer, Sage*; and I also teach it to my clients and students in Butterfly Circle.

- Listen to Solfreggio Frequencies to clear your energetic field of disturbances to your true alignment, and raise up the vibration of your energy body to a level where it is easier to download messages psychically.

- Ground your energy body by standing barefoot on the Earth for 15 minutes a day, sitting with your back against a tree, or listening to a grounding meditation.

- Shield your energy body to prevent interference from other signals. You can guide yourself in the shielding process, or listen to a guided shielding mediation.

- Take deep cleansing breaths throughout your day to flush your system of stress and restore peace and tranquility.

- Balance your nervous system by placing one hand over heart, the other over belly, and doing deep breathing with your eyes closed for five minutes.

- Practice yoga, chi-gong, or breathwork to get the energy moving in your physical and subtle bodies and elevate your overall vibration. Breath of fire is one kundalini yoga practice I learned from The Four Winds Society and also share with my clients and students.

- Open sacred space around yourself as you begin your day to welcome the Great Spirit into the flow of events, and cultivate a nighttime ritual for relaxation and reclaiming energy so that you are able to sleep well at night.

- If you find yourself having sleep challenges, explore a reduction in caffeine during the day.

- Commit to some form of meditation practice every day to bring yourself to a space of inner quiet and spaciousness into which can float information you require for your day. Messages from Great Spirit and your guides come in the quiet spaciousness between the things and doings.

- Commit to regular weekly exercise outdoors in nature to allow yourself to immerse in the frequencies of other forms of life which will assist you in clearing your channel.

- Drink plenty of non-fluoridated water every day. Pay attention to the source of your water and how it arrives in your glass. Get a filtration system and consider placing intention into your water before you drink it.

- Regularly perform energy cleansing of your space, especially where you sleep. I recommend that my clients and students claim their space by installing a crystal grid and making certain invocations, and then using burning sage to clear the space of any distractions. Bells, chimes and chants are also great ways to elevate the energy of your surroundings.

♥

Stop Trying To Blend In. Shine!

You're not here to act the same as everyone else, nor are you here to be liked. You're here to access that clear channel to a higher way of living and be the example through demonstration. As you shine, you will attract lower vibratory patterns from the people in your life, and bubble them up within yourself, so those shadows can be witnessed in the light. Don't take it personally! You're doing a perfect job if you're stirring up difficult feelings in others by shining your light. The denser energy born of history is being witnessed, and what we are aware of we can change by making a new choice. Part of your purpose is to make the invisible…visible. As you do so, you transition the egoic Personality self, little by little, into a different relationship with your soul. So of course, in a world driven by ego, many people will be disturbed by your words, actions and presence because you're rattling the egoic cage just be being yourself in your higher vibration.

You may resist stepping into your purpose out of a fear of being seen. Partly this resistance is fear generated by a historical resonance in the collective consciousness from persecution of people whose spirituality was Earth-centric. You may have had a lifetime of being burned at the stake as a witch, or having your tribe murdered as an indigenous person, or being attacked for your religious beliefs, or some variation of this theme; you may also just be tuned into the resonance of this pattern in the collective consciousness. Do your inner work to discern the source of resistance and fear within you and clear it. Encourage yourself to keep stepping to the edge of discomfort and past it into greater and greater exposure. Each fear you encounter along the way is something you can transform, overcome, and become the embodied healing of.

There are aspects of self that prefer you to remain hidden. Mainly I speak of the child self within who potentially experienced some form of rejection when shining her authentic light. Moving into greater exposure is a dance with the Inner Child where you demonstrate protection and safety with every step into the light. It's an inner negotiation that is ongoing as you expand your light in the world. Ultimately, your Inner Child requires your love, attention, and protection. The degree to which you provide this to your Inner Child is the degree to which your purpose work will flourish.

You are also invited to shift from the conditioning of the collective which has trained you to require the validation from others to be in your knowing. You are invited to find all the answers you require for your particular soul journey from your own clear channel to the Divine. Tune into **your** station and let go of your conditioned need for someone to tell you that you are doing it right, or heard the message correctly. Only by fully embracing the clear message flowing through your station will you be able to confidently disrupt historical patterns and deliver new vibratory patterns to your human systems.

Up until now, you may have felt alone and isolated. Now you have the opportunity to gift yourself support in the community of other Second Wave volunteers. It's amazing how a little bit of community support can nurture your light into shining exponentially brighter.

You are in this world, but not of this world. You are meant to be a lighthouse in the darkness. Shine!

♥

Suggestions

Become Your Own Proof Our Western minds are trained to want 'proof' of something before investing time and energy into it. Dismantle this egoic mental structure by introducing curiosity and experiments into your spiritual practice. There are many suggestions in the chapter you just read. Go back through and pick a couple of suggestions to try out over a week or a month. Be your own expert and decide whether that suggestion makes a beneficial impact in your life. Let go of one-size-fits-all thinking and embrace the possibility that the Great Spirit has a unique life plan laid out specifically for you. Welcome the adventure!

Keep Releasing Judgment We have been conditioned to judge other people and ourselves rather than simply be curious. Judgment is one of the ways that the egoic Self maintains control...by creating separation. When you become aware of yourself in judgment, write down the thought on a strip of paper, blow into it how that thought makes you feel, and burn it with fire which is a cleansing and transformation energy. Notice how you feel. Does that judgment subside in your consciousness? What if you keep burning the thought whenever you notice it. Does it stop coming to mind and disappear? This can be a very interesting experiment to run.

What's In Your Shadow About Shining? Encourage yourself to step out in a greater way and shine your light. Then notice the inner dialog. What do the voices in your head tell you? How does your body react to the idea of being seen in a bigger way? Use your tools to clear this energy so you can expand even further into purpose.

Charting the Course Out Of Madness

As I began opening to my spiritual journey and leading my life from higher consciousness, I became 'woo' and 'crazy' in the eyes of many people around me. Where once I used to live in the same world as them, running around distracted and disconnected, I now was beginning to see that the world I used to live in was actually the one that was crazy. In the world most people consider reality, it's hard to connect with spiritual people, or people who found Jesus, who seem happy to be alive and filled up with some kind of drug that makes them glow. No, in the normal world you've got to keep a tight grip to stay on top of the teeming masses. You can't lose control for a minute or reveal your weaknesses because your survival is entirely dependent on your ability to outrun everyone else.

The more I ventured into my spiritual practices, the more crust I removed from my Divine Spark, and the more I realized how sane, loving, compassionate, and beautiful my life was becoming. I experienced an expansion of time, space, and self-compassion. I found I could relax for hours meditating, and then accomplish my work goals in a flow that seemed beyond time. My heart overflowed with love and joy...this was not crazy. This was incredible. At some point it became clear to me that the reality most people live in is 'Upside Down World', and to turn the world 'Right Side Up' you've got to remove the crust. To chart the course out of madness I had to dismantle my personality to make room for my soul.

We discussed the crust that forms around the Divine Spark and how it filters a person's perceptions according to its matrix. The matrix of crust is comprised of a person's ancestral DNA, early childhood experiences which established operational belief structures, programming from the collective consciousness, and egoic structures formed in self-protection. Each of these crust factories contributes to the rich experience of being human, while at the same time restricting access to one's Divine Spark and higher consciousness connection.

The message I hear from the Great Spirit is that the Earth is a relatively new planet who chose her own incarnation goals, and so this has been a grand experiment to see what happens when there is a conscious species that goes into a lifetime with amnesia and free will governed by the laws of karma and attraction.

The human crust is chosen by the incarnating soul to guarantee that the soul will experience a certain set of conditions which the soul has chosen to learn from. Otherwise, wouldn't you certainly avoid your lessons once in a human body? If you remained conscious that you selected to be raped in this lifetime, would you willingly go into the experience? I think we all know the answer, given how people resist their lessons even while being consciously unaware of them. Luckily, you're born into a body that has the Ancestral DNA and environmental conditions to support you into stumbling into your lessons completely unconscious. Beyond this, the very moment and location you're born lends you a human design type that also governs your life experience and further assists you to take the journey your soul selected.

Selecting conditions is like selecting classes at school. This is why 'Earth School' is a very adequate metaphor for the life experience on Earth. For example, a soul might have karma in a lifetime from raping a person, and therefore in this lifetime, the soul selected to experience the classroom on being raped. Everything in Earth School must balance out to zero. The famous epithet "Do unto others as you would have them do unto you" is this teaching about the way karma works. It is very good advice, and meant to help you consciously create in a way that serves your highest good, rather than creating in a way that drags you into more lifetimes to resolve karma. Of course, you are at free will to create whatever you choose on Earth, and this freedom comes at the cost of reciprocity: everything must balance to neutral in the end. You cannot leave Earth School until your balance is zeroed out. This is a collective agreement with the divine being Gaia, Mother Earth, so that she is not left to clean up the mess for souls incarnating to this planet to create from free will.

Up until now, as a result of these Earth constructs, human history is rife with conflict because souls have been immersed in the human crust without the benefit of the higher consciousness that the Divine Spark brings. Making soul progress on Earth has been challenging and slow because of this immersion in human crust; without the guidance of the Divine Spark, a soul can get sucked into karma quicksand for lifetimes. While this has been the excuse for making slow progress on soul lessons up until now, humans on Earth no longer have that excuse with the Aquarian Age.

We are at a time in human history where it behooves us to remove crust so we can operate with one foot in the human, one foot in the Spirit, and navigate life keeping both alive at the same time. Clearing the human crust makes it possible for us to live with open empathic hearts feeling it all, while also enjoying the peace and neutrality of being a witness to the human theatre. That is why the Second Wave of volunteers is here: to demonstrate through personal example how to rise up from Earth amnesia, clear the human crust, and operate with one foot in both worlds. There can be egoic resistance to recognizing Divine consciousness because once you know better, you have to do better. Also because many people fear facing the backlog of unwitnessed sewage that's necessary to undergo as part of the cleansing process. Indeed, it is a time of reckoning; but this does not have to be hard. It can be fascinating.

To understand the human crust better, let us take each of the contributing factors in turn and elaborate on how they help to form the crust around the Divine Spark, and how that impacts a person's clarity of perception.

♥

The Power of Ancestral DNA in Your Body

Ancestral DNA essentially means that the experiences of your ancestors live on through your cellular memory, which means it seems like the thoughts and feelings stemming from that ancestral memory belong to you. You can feel it in your body, and that feels personal. I'll tell you a story to illustrate the point. When I was searching for my Cherokee roots, I went to the Cherokee nation in the Smoky Mountains seeking answers. One stop I made was to the Museum of the Cherokee Nation and asked at the front desk if there was someone who could help me locate my great-great-grandmother in the rolls, or if there was another way beyond the veil to connect with her. The young man at the counter that I asked was full-blooded Cherokee from Oklahoma; his ancestors had survived the trauma of the Trail of Tears to make it to the reservation in Oklahoma. When I mentioned that my ancestor had left the people and married a Caucasian man because she could pass for white, he said to me "She left the people. She was a traitor, and traitors are not accepted back into the tribe."

These words stung me deeply. It felt like every cell in my body lit up with fury; my blood boiled, I felt my face flush, and I felt a fire rage through my core. I've never experienced such a visceral anger than I did in this moment. It took me by surprise. I felt shame, guilt, judgment, hate, grief: all of this swarming throughout every cell of my body. I walked away from the young man stunned and into the exhibit hall where I took some deep breaths and grounded myself. I needed to understand why I was having such a powerful reaction. After all, it wasn't me that had done these things or lived this lifetime. It wasn't me that was being rejected by her people. But in a way it was.

As I tracked these sensations within myself and listened for messages, I felt my ancestors calling to me "No one can take your blood from you." Standing in the museum in front of human replicas of Cherokee people, I wept. The grief was overwhelming. Far greater than any rational reason I had to be upset. It became clear to me that this grief belonged to my great-great-grandmother: the grief of losing her family and people to have a better life. And I realized it was her rage I felt: anger at her great-great-granddaughter not being acknowledged for her Cherokee blood. I allowed the grief and anger to wash over me and release. I began to feel the welcoming arms of my Cherokee ancestors beyond the veil.

Having had this personal embodied experience of my ancestral DNA, I found I was now able to spot this pattern in my clients. Clients would come to me with a conscious desire to behave in one way, and an unconscious (almost gravitational) pull to do the opposite. As I talked with them and explored their inner matrix, we would find the ancestral root for their current unconscious pattern and clear it. The client would then be relieved of the impediment of the unconscious pull towards the undesired behavior, and be able to move forward towards their desired outcomes.

There are many ways to explore the subconscious, which stores ancestral experiences, and clear the root of ancestral trauma and outdated programming. My methodology involves using the imagination in a sacred space construct called The Sanctuary, and calling forth the ancestor who created the root of the program during their time on Earth. Then through a process of healing the past, the client is able to clear her DNA of the program, effectively healing herself through epigenetics. With epigenetics, we can change the expression of the gene code that lives in a person's DNA structure, inherited from their ancestry. Changing the expression of the gene code changes the person's human crust, thereby changing the person's energetic signature and perceptual filters to present an entirely fresh outcome, free of the past.

Can you imagine how I might have reacted to the young man at the Cherokee Museum if I had not had a level of awareness that told me to stop and look within? In other words, if I did not have access to the guidance of my higher consciousness? I would have thought that he made me feel rage and grief by his words, because I was feeling it in my body. I would have felt attacked by him, and been tempted to retaliate, or gossip about the experience and project blame and judgment onto him. As it was, even with access to the knowing I received, I cast a glare at him on my way out of the museum hours later. This is how powerful ancestral DNA is in the body. It stirs up storms of emotions that, with consciousness, we can understand as a cry from our ancestors to bring healing.

As part of the Second Wave, your service is to become aware of the triggers of ancestral DNA that live within you and heal through epigenetics. An added service is to take timely opportunities to make others aware of the potential that their body might be revealing ancestral wounds to them. What is meant by 'timely opportunities' are those moments where the person is open and welcoming of hearing a possibility they have not yet considered. When sharing this potential with others, a personal story is extremely helpful because it illustrates the point by demonstration. Demonstration and storytelling is how the Second Wave volunteers will best communicate these principles to the people we meet.

♥

The Foundation of Early Childhood Experiences

Much has been written about how early childhood experiences impact the developing mind of a child. So I will share with you here what I have personally discovered that complements this wealth of insight already available to you through other sources.

Many other teachings of the effect of early childhood on a person cover the external aspects that any person can readily witness. Something traumatic happens that the child sees, or it happens to the child, and that trauma gets stored in the body memory, sometimes resurfacing later in life. Or the family always repeats a story about the child, cementing in that identity for the child: "you're the smart one", "you're the athletic one", "you're the wild one." Or the child has an interaction and makes a choice that gets embedded in the framework of their mind and it starts gaining momentum.

One example of an unconscious childhood choice impacting your life is my earliest memory of watching my second step father Fred playing a guitar. I was around 3 years old. He stopped playing, put the guitar on the bed, and told me not to touch it. As soon as he left the room, I reached my hand up and touched it and the strings made a noise. He came rushing back in and hit me, and I ran crying to my mother who was cooking ground beef in the skillet in the kitchen. This fully sensory memory stuck with me because I made an important choice in the moment of this incident: It's not safe to play. It took a subconscious healing modality called Constellations to unpack for me the meaning of this early memory so that I could know I made the choice "It's not safe to play." Of course, I had spent my life proving it was safe to play, all the while fighting a foundational belief to the contrary.

What gets tricky with early childhood foundational agreements is that some of these decisions are made unconsciously before a child even has words. The decisions could even be made in utero! This is why traditional psychotherapy is largely ineffective with accessing foundational psychological structures. There aren't words for some of these belief structures, so talking about it in a literal way never gets to the root of it.

I hope this section reveals another whole depth to the conversation of early childhood cognitive structures: the psychic-energetic relationship between mother and child, the relationship dynamics between the child's natural parents, the ongoing spoken and unspoken attitudes and beliefs, the energetic and emotional dependencies, and the unresolved traumas of the parents all play a very significant part in cultivation of a child's human crust.

The crust of early childhood experiences starts forming in utero, before the baby is even born. The baby begins learning from its host, the mother, immediately through feeling. The first organ to develop in a baby is the heart, and this is because the heart 'brain' is the most complex and fundamental of human organs. The heart has access to the Divine Spark, Source, and the wealth of information stored in the subconscious auric field of the developing fetus including past lives, soul incarnation objectives, and more that the Great Spirit indicates is not relevant for this discussion.

I do know that one can travel through a special doorway in the heart for shamanic journey and enter a portal into other dimensions of existence. Anyone who has been to one of my drum journeys has experienced this capacity of their hearts. It's pretty magical to know that you have everything you need right inside of you to understand yourself multi-dimensionally.

Back to the subject at hand, in my own experience of being a mother twice, I felt the soul presence of my first son very clearly inside my womb. I remember when his presence became palpable, and I could feel him tuning into me. This was a powerful enough experience to break through my crust because I did not have my awakening from Earth amnesia until about 13 years later. I could feel him learning from me, his consciousness actively exploring my consciousness. I was teaching him and with every thought, every feeling, every bodily sensation, and every external event I was experiencing outside of my body. Instinctively, I did my best to be positive and not be overcome by my usual bouts of anger or depression.

Still, when he was born, all he did for months was cry. We could find nothing wrong with him: no diaper rash, no pinching clothes, and nothing to cause an upset tummy. He was often inconsolable, even if he was pushed for miles in a stroller.

In retrospect I see several truths that have surfaced over and over again in the course of his life:

- There was a lot of unhealed karma in both his father's ancestry and my own that he was personally grappling with on his journey.
- There were toxic dynamics in the relationship between his father and myself that needed healing, and these dynamics were affecting him in his body.
- My first son is a Second Wave volunteer and his function by human design type is to be a healer. His senses are refined and sensitive; he feels it all, and he's psychically open and aware.

Raising my sons has helped me to see many of my own early childhood dynamics. Similar to my sons, there was a lot of unhealed karma in my father's ancestry as well as what I inherited from my mother. There were toxic dynamics in the relationship between my biological parents, and there was trauma and toxicity in the relationship between my mother and first step-father that I witnessed. Throughout my life, I could feel my mother's resentment and disdain for my natural father as a kind of deep dislike of me personally. When she started to project this disdain onto my second son when he was a child, that's when I saw the pattern clearly and remembered how she had always expressed those similar fears when I was a child: that I would 'turn out' just like my natural father who she considered to be a sexual deviant. The war between my natural parents was alive in my life even though they had not seen each other since I was 2 years old. The distance didn't matter. The DNA in my very cells told the truth. The resonance of my natural father lived on within my own body, provoking and triggering her resentment at an unconscious level.

Another story I wish to share with you will illustrate the power of the resonance of the 'other parent' in your body. This story will seem a bit 'woo' for some of you who are just now awakening, but give it a sliver of potentiality and you may see a profound truth. I met my natural father, Jack, when I was a first-year student in college. My mother helped to arrange the visit and even accompanied me to see him. I saw him several times the first three years of college until he passed away from AIDS the year I graduated. The relationship with my natural father felt very unresolved because I had felt threatened by his penetrating gaze and certainly felt my mother's disdain rippling through my cells.

Because my mother was my only consistent parent until I was 5 years old when we met my Dad (my second step-father), our energy bodies became very entwined. We were wrapped up in each other. It was us against the world. Together we had survived physical and emotional abuse, and my mom had saved me from a life of child molestation. We were trapped on the Triangle of Disempowerment, being victims and rescuers of each other against the perpetrators. It was like I did not have a voice of my own, or would not claim my own ground to stand on. I remember feeling like my mother's defender, rather than protected by her. My mother confirms my warrior spirit with stories from my childhood like the time I stood up in the car when another driver was bothering her, and shook my fist and yelled. I share this experience to help you make the connection to your own story. The Second Wave soul can feel the responsibility to rescue others, and have the sense that he or she has the innate power to help, even from early childhood. The Second Wave soul can also become absorbed by the beliefs and opinions of others, finding it hard to find his or her own voice.

While my natural father was alive, trying to connect with him while being very energetically and emotionally entwined with my mother proved to be challenging. After his death I felt relieved but also sad because I never was able to bring myself to love him the way I thought I should. One day walking in downtown Northampton, my college town, I glanced behind me and saw him clear as day, big grin on his face. I blinked my eyes and he was gone.

Over the course of the next year a number of uncharacteristic things happened. I cheated on my loving boyfriend of 6 years, we broke up, and I spontaneously decided to move across the country to San Francisco where I had never been. Within one month I had an affair with my roommate, got a natural consequence of sexual promiscuity (I contracted herpes), and then met my future husband. I moved in with Tom six months later and when my parents came to visit me they said "Who are you? You are not the daughter we used to know."

And so began a long period of strained relations with my parents which only got more difficult when my former husband and I moved to Texas where they were living. Moving to Texas and being in close proximity to my mother seemed to activate another sequence in my life where I began acting out by being sexually promiscuous. Psychotherapy revealed early childhood trauma that was unresolved and instigating rebellious behavior, and if I had mentored myself at this time, I would have gone straight to ancestral trauma and childhood healing.

Flash forward to the end of my marriage and more family drama that severed relations with my mother and Dad for awhile, but led me to explore healing modalities that were essential for my soul development and mission. As part of my healing I attended the Four Winds Light Body School where we learned about entities and how sometimes when people die, they go to the 'light'...but it's not the right 'light.' During my healing with four students assisting, I witnessed the extraction of my natural father from my body both externally by watching the students track his entity and move it out of me, and internally as I finally felt the differentiation of his presence within me and realized 'who' it was they were extracting. After they extracted him, I felt a huge emptiness inside of me. I became highly aware that I had only been taking up half of the space within me.

The realization that my natural father's essence had been inside of me the whole time since his death was profound. In the absence of him, I expanded to take up the entire space of my being. I was so much calmer without him, and was no longer sexually promiscuous. I was also not as much 'fun' in the way that he was fun. Questions rose in my mind like "Would I have ever done what I did if Jack had not hopped on board my being?" There were too many tiny realizations to mention here, but suffice it to say that my entire energetic resonance changed after his extraction from my being. My mom and Dad and I were able to reconnect and that meant the world to me. They remarked that I seemed like my old self. It was a profound insight about how the resonance of the 'other parent' can damage your relationship with your child because of your own unresolved baggage.

There's so much that could be said here about the ways that the open sponge of a child's mind can be influenced in nuanced, often undetected ways, to form a crust over the Divine Spark. The more traumatic the experiences, the thicker the crust that gets formed because the child feels the need to protect itself. We'll discuss more about that in the *Protected By Egoic Structures* section.

I hope the stories and ideas expressed in this section have given you a launching point for your own investigation into your early childhood. We are entering a new frontier of human consciousness and awareness, so you are invited to be an explorer. The time of relying on 'experts' to tell you what to say or do is coming to an end. While certainly people who have studied a subject extensively can offer sage guidance, the encouragement is to realize that all humans are embarking on a new discovery with the Age of Aquarius which is leveling the playing field.

Additionally, consider that institutionalized information born of historical structures and consciousness may no longer be relevant going forward. If a modality doesn't help you rise above the human crust, or at least navigate it effectively to make progress towards heart-opening and expansion of your consciousness, it may not be serving your highest good. Institutions are created by humans, and humans have crust. Without clarity and guidance from higher realms of consciousness, an institution is only as effective as the ability of the humans who created it to navigate their inner crust. So who can you trust? Trust your intuition to guide you to the teachers who can assist you in accessing your own inner truth, and be willing to go on the resulting adventure.

♥

Healing Our Ancestors Seven Generations Forward and Back

As I've mentioned throughout this book, the Second Wave volunteers have come to embody human DNA and heal ancestral patterns through epigenetics so that we resolve old karmas that run down the family line. When we heal an old ancestral karma that lives on in our DNA, we ripple that healing back seven generations, and we liberate our children from carrying out the suffering in their own lives today.

I've spoken about the power of ancestral karma in your DNA to impact your ability to make a new choice for yourself today that's more appropriate for your life. Until you've experienced the gravitational pull of these ancestral patterns in your own life, it can be hard to relate. Throughout my life, I have been very capable of overcoming challenges. For example, several times I gained weight, but then applied myself through will power to lose up to 65 pounds over the course of six to eight months. I also ran two marathons and over a dozen half marathons, dedicating myself to miles of weekly training to prepare my body. Organizationally, I led over 200 artists in the Bay Area of California to open their studios to the public over three weekends in May—a monumental task of volunteer cooperation, media publicity, and collateral production. Those are just some examples of how I've been the kind of person that can 'get shit done.'

So when I was drawn into the unthinkable scenario of a love affair with my first cousin before my awakening, and was unable to resist it (in fact, was obsessed with it), I was shocked with myself. How could I engage in that dynamic which I know is not good for myself, my children, my marriage, or my extended family? I spun off into a dark night of the soul where I became a person I did not recognize. Traditional psychotherapy could not help me process this madness; all it could do was give me a label of borderline personality disorder and tell me I was innately flawed. (My memoir, *"Awakening To Me: One Woman's Journey To Self Love"* is a recounting of the early part of my awakening process.)

As I embarked on my journey of awakening, I came to understand that my unexpected behavior was actually part of a larger context of child abuse and molestation that ran down my natural father's ancestral line. I also became aware that my natural father had joined my conscious journey as an entity within me. And I came to learn about how families are farmed by energetic parasites, and provoked into behaviors designed to generate the desired output: fear, anger, shame, hate, and so forth. Had I been aware of the possibility of being impacted by these forces in my own mind and body, I might have identified my urges as something bigger than my own self and gotten the kind of help that would have broken the pattern: epigenetics healing.

There are many unconscious patterns of behavior in our lives that skate under the surface of our awareness, and are inherited from our ancestry. Many of dynamics in your life (desired and undesired) are a product of ancestral inheritance. When we become aware of an ancestral pattern and try to change it through thinking and will power, it can be very difficult to overcome because of the gravitational energetic pull of the pattern in our own bodies, thoughts, and emotions. But when you can break the energetic pull of the ancestral pattern—which expresses itself in your thoughts, emotions and body sensations—you get the relief you need to shift the pattern with your will.

Many ancestral dynamics affect your relationship with family members. The ancestral pattern can be thought of like Velcro; you have one part of the Velcro, the family member has the other part. As you become aware of the ancestral dynamic and heal it within yourself, you remove your part of the Velcro; in other words, you erase the energetic pull of the ancestral pattern from your being. At this point, the other family member can still have their Velcro, but there's nothing sticky in you anymore for that pattern so it has no charge. With no charge, the family member begins making subtle unconscious changes that remove the dynamic between you; potentially this family member unconsciously seeks out another family member with whom to play out the dynamic.

You can assist with the dissipation of the ancestral dynamic within your family by healing the pattern within yourself and energetically transmitting the upgraded DNA to other family members; this happens naturally without you doing anything but being in the presence of other family members. You can also assist the dissipation of the ancestral dynamic within your family by being the demonstration of new, higher vibration patterns of communication and behavior. You cannot, however, force family members to realign themselves energetically or behaviorally to the new, higher vibrational patterns. Each person has free will, and chooses his or her own pathways to ascension (or more karma).

During an epigenetics healing that incorporates your ancestors, it's possible to heal the pattern back to the root where it started...even if the root trauma occurred generations ago. Whether you heal a pattern that got started in your childhood, or one that began with your great-

great-grandmother, the shift of the pattern at the root of the trauma cascades as a healing force that uplifts the entire timeline. We can't change the event that occurred, but we can shift the energy that's been held about it and carried forward through the lineage. We can change the vibratory patterns from suffering to wisdom which is a much more empowering legacy to pass along.

Can you imagine the ripple effect of healing an ancestral trauma that began with an ancestor three generations back? Looking backwards through your ancestry, you can extrapolate all the lives affected by the healing of that one pattern, including yourself; and then look forward to imagine how that healing will bless all future generations in your family.

Are you starting to understand the profound impact of a Second Wave volunteer on the human story? Can you leave behind the feelings of self-pity and 'why did this happen to me', and embrace the power of your own healing journey for shifting the lives of your ancestors and loved ones? Do you see how all the healing you've done on yourself so far has had a profound ripple effect?

Now I introduce a good friend to share his wisdom with you, Gary Stuart. Gary Stuart is a personal development expert of 45 years and a Master Constellation Healing facilitator of over 20+ years. He's the creator of the innovative *Constellation Healing Oracle Card* deck. He's also an author of *Ancestral Intelligence: Constellation Insights from Beyond* with a companion Guided Journal. His other books include *Master YOUR Universe: How to Direct & Start in YOUR Own Life* plus *Many Hearts ONE SOUL*.

♥

Ancestral Intelligence by Gary Stuart

We are all here because our ancestors' lineage made good choices. In hindsight it's easy to judge (we all do). Life throws us an infinite variety of challenges. Whether the challenges are good or bad, functional or dysfunctional, we are forced to rise to the occasion in the same way as they did. Of course their daily lives, based on historical events of the generational timeline, were very different than ours. We often think we're different, yet we're all very much the same. Everyone alive tries to make the best choice possible in any given time. At the very least we believe we are doing so making us no different than those who came before. At the very worst we have to live through the consequences and the outcome of our choices.

Life seems to demand that we exist in a constant state of change. Chi, or life force, wouldn't have it any other way. You could say the one constant of the universe is adapt or die. This this seems to be life's greatest demand which includes all living things from amoebas to aquatic life and insects to flowers and fauna and animals, and of course human beings as well. Each species has its own challenges to survive each and every day. Some days getting food is easier than other days; any moment it could be your last second to be alive. Life's instructions are to eat or be eaten, killed or be killed; this is an inherent evolutionary rule which you could call the price of being alive. Even our neurochemistry with how we process fear, fight or flight at the deepest cellular level shows every living thing is wired the same way to survive.

In human family systems another curveball was added to the mix in our quest for survival. Human beings of every race color and creed have personal emotions and beliefs. This also applies to dramas and traumas played out in human history by nations, societies, and globally, which makes life even more complex. In family systems we see each generational response to life and its challenges is psychologically and epigenetically recorded, then transmitted to the next generation of descendants as a way to ensure their survival. We exist right now at this present moment because what I call "Ancestral Intelligence" that was passed down from your forebears to you.

The good news, and not so good news, is they also passed down the baggage of negative beliefs and patterns too. These messages were transmitted to the descendants as limitations and warnings from a time and place that no longer exists.

A healing modality called the Constellation healing process unlocks the energy behind the family history and many of its secrets. We often see family systems that are rife with incest, sexual abuse and violence. It's almost as if our forebears had the same experience, so they repeat the behavior on the unsuspecting descendants as your forebears did to them. I know it doesn't make logical sense but it's a generational repetition and sharing of pain which ironically unites and bonds everyone in the same dysfunctional experience while they have the inherited family gift of being alive. If that's not a paradox I don't know what is.

As any dysfunctional behavior spreads over generations, the suffering continues into the future until some descendants have the courage to heal and break the chain of suffering. There's often a price of rejection when any family member becomes disloyal to the insanity or suffering by their own family or outside forces. Of course, those outside forces perpetuated the suffering which your family members reacted to during their lifetime. It takes courage to challenge the very system that gave you the gift of life. Most families feel it's a small price to pay. Belonging to your family system by inheriting its pain makes it a conundrum to even want to belong to any family system. It's not an easy task to change or heal but it is possible.

I found in my 20 years of Constellation healing facilitation that life doesn't judge right or wrong, good or bad or evil. It seems like life is always neutral and that it's the societies that perpetuate right and wrong, good or bad, moral and amoral—mostly through religion and many other societal beliefs that limit human experience to give them more power. It seems that these organizations put pressure on everyone to be the same. Control is maintained by excluding other religions or colors or creeds to make the religion appear divine by being the only voice heard. Over the centuries, religion has excluded homosexuals, lesbians, trans, bi children to name a few. Lest we forget that misogyny against females with domestic violence and abuse also plays a part in this patriarchal domination of everything on the planet including Mother Earth herself who's currently being raped by corporate parasites that are draining and polluting her

CHARTING THE COURSE OUT OF MADNESS

resources to the point of mass extinction for temporary profits. I won't even go into the ongoing genocide of indigenous peoples globally. As we know human history is rife with millions of injustices against innocent people in the name of the God by people who think God is on their side and justifying their behavior at great cost to anything outside their system of belief.

In family systems we find repetition of disease expressed by different emotions that seem to dominate the mindset of the family system. There can be a poverty mindset due to loyalty to poverty, or a wealth mindset due to successes. Many religious texts promise you'll be closer to God if you're poor and suffering only to be rewarded in heaven after you leave hell on Earth. This dogma is mind control at its worst. All of this history is part of our ancestral mix, yet we juggle it all in the many dynamics we experience in everyday life while simultaneously being part of human history. Got drama, anyone?

In some ways we can escape; yet there is no escape. Remember, it's all about change as I said earlier: "adapt or die." Everyone alive seems to be forced to comply with the rules of the family or nation into which they are born. The negative side of our Ancestral Intelligence is that the dysfunctional experiences are then passed down as suffering. Many inherit pain and exclusion not to mention the sexual insanity perpetrated by religious institutions that were once considered sacred. This proves that everything and everyone is fallible, and no Pope or crucifix can cover up this truth. It's ironic that the clergy is corrupting unsuspecting believers who pay for salvation and redemption to be closer to God. "Forgive me father I have sinned" should start with the church globally. Most families adopt some kind of religious standard unknowingly creating generational pain and suffering. Many use "God is on their side" to justify genocide, slavery for generation after generation, and killing anyone and everything in the way for alleged glory. Now it's the church's time to "adapt or die."

Spiritual people are people who do not believe in organized religion and have been shunned or maligned for centuries. Many non-believers were even murdered for their pagan beliefs that religious organizations co-opted as their own. Many fail to question how the ancient stories were changed over time to suit the needs of the church. Most people who believe in their doctrines do not think for themselves because thinking for yourself is not encouraged in dogmatic systems.

When you look at human history through the lens of objectivity, you see that humanity has always been living in a feudal system. Call it what you will but it's essentially monarchy, royalty or political aristocracy. You can call it a government democracy, communism, fascism or even tribalism. They all share one thing in common: they are right, and God is on their side. If you doubt this, just look at world history with all the wars, genocide and killing throughout human history, done in the name of "my God is better than your God." It seems Life doesn't really care. Humanity still grows and evolves even if it's fed by death and destruction. Hinduism covers this very succinctly. Life itself will go on and on into infinity with or without human beings. We need her more than she needs us. Life has one goal: to move forward at all cost and never look back.

What do we have here? Our human history demonstrates that our species evolves with endless patterns of change, adaptation and growth. Even in the face of the aforementioned atrocities committed against many peoples trying to survive, we are still here. Therefore, no matter what time of history we live in: everything is a gift. Can we make the most of it and change the course of our life, and thereby change the course of human history? Yes!

We can choose to evolve our own life during our time on Earth. We have always had the power if we choose to use it. This is our birthright. Everyone alive represents the hope of our ancestors for a better future on Earth. It's often said by Native Americans and First People that everything we do today reflects seven generations behind us and seven generations in front of us. This also was even spoken in biblical texts as "the sins of the father fall on the sons."

Everyone inherited LIFE as a gift and a burden too. The million-dollar question is can we let the past be the past and not repeat the mistakes of our ancestors? I say "Yes!" Using Constellation healing we can alter the future course of our own history as well as heal the histories of those who came before us. The key is to accept that everything is a gift, even the past and all its imperfections, and to deeply understand that you are here because of what came before. Ancestral Intelligence has served you well.

It's your choice. Do you have the courage to accept the gift as it came to you and leave whatever's not the gift back in the past? This is called acceptance of life the way it is and was. In doing so, you gain the freedom to make your life what YOU want it to be. Let the negative experiences of history rest with your forebears. Let them be placed behind you in the collective past with a sense of honor and respect. It's your turn to make your dreams come true. This is your birthright as it was theirs in their time.

When you manifest your ideal life for yourself, you do it for all who came before you and all who come after you: 7 generations in either direction. The present moment is your point of power, POP! If you have the courage to evolve your consciousness, you'll create a new pattern in the present for the future. Personal freedom and actualization can then be yours.

♥

From Victim to Epigenetic Artist

Up until now, you may have felt victimized by your life's experiences and how your family treated you. In your heart you've always known what it should have been like, how you should have been loved and supported. As Gary Stuart shared with us, holding onto resentments and judgments for your parents and ancestors only serves to keep you entangled in the dynamics of suffering. If you're tangled up in the family patterns with charged emotions, you're very likely to repeat them in your own life and spread them to your own children.

The solution is to liberate yourself through understanding and forgiveness, and become an artist of your epigenetics. You may have inherited traumas and patterns of suffering in the cells of your body, but guess what? As you bring your Divinity into your cellular structures, you can become the artist of your own epigenetics. You get to set a new vision for yourself and your children from the place of embodied Divinity. How cool is that?

Part of the rewiring is to step off the Triangle of Disempowerment which has three anchored roles: perpetrator, victim, and rescuer. If you play any of these roles in your life, you are anchored to the Triangle and you are disempowered from your full sovereignty. I help clients and students become liberated from this human program energetically and cognitively. An aspect of the cognitive disentanglement is to admit the ways you have occupied all three anchored roles on the Triangle. If you've played one role, you've played them all. Only by 'fessing up' and forgiving yourself and others can you be free.

Another part of the rewiring is facing all your feelings about these patterns of suffering. When emotional energy is trapped in the body through suppression, it remains active in your epigenetics like a signal beeping out into the word: 'send me more of this suffering.' If you are triggered by something, there are trapped emotions that need release. Your mind may argue 'but I've healed that already'; your feelings tell you the truth. The only way out of the darkness is through the feelings; you've got to feel it to transform it.

Yet another aspect of the rewiring is accepting that some of the trauma you're feeling in your body isn't 'yours'; it comes from the experiences of your ancestors. You're part of the family system and inherit its goodness and its not-so-goodness, as Gary Stuart shared with us. Perhaps your ancestry faced wars and genocide, and now you get to offer your service in cleaning up the expression of it in your epigenetics so it doesn't keep perpetuating in your own life and your childrens'. Maybe you have ancestors who were slave-owners, and you feel guilty or angry when facing this topic of discussion; an ancestral healing can really unlock this energy for the benefit of yourself and countless others.

See the human traumas for what they really are: programs of human suffering. Become objective about it like a programmer of your own computer system. If you do not like the program of <fill in the blank>, then do the energetic and cognitive processing to wipe this program off your computer system. As you remove it from the expression of your epigenetics, your life begins expressing in new, healthy ways. Doing this work is a gift to yourself, your children, and your children's children.

As you heal these patterns within yourself, and forgive those who came before you, you also are encouraged to be mindful around your Welcome mat. Healing ancestral wounds does not require you to sacrifice your own health and happiness. If someone in your family is treating you poorly, then set a loving boundary and do the inner work to clear the energy within yourself and restore your peace. As much as we do not want to return negative volleys with another person, we also are not being asked to martyr ourselves by continuing to receive toxic energy from a person who is choosing to act in hurtful ways. A loving boundary is practicing non-engagement with wounded dynamics, avoiding projections and gossip, doing inner work to heal within Self, and practicing forgiveness. Notice how all of that happens without the involvement of the other person.

♥

Parenting a Second or Third Wave Child

If you are blessed to be the parent of a Second Wave or Third Wave child, let me share a few realizations that might empower you to gift your child with a greater legacy than you previously imagined was possible.

- Regardless of whether you read this before you birth a child, or long after, it is imperative that you do your part to clear ancestral patterns from your DNA so as to reduce the burden of these dynamics on your child. It's never too late because 'time' is just a construct. It's all happening now. This means you must focus on your own healing as a priority. It is not selfish. It's the most generous thing you can do for your children.

- Heal your relationship with your child's father/mother. As your children grow, they feel the karma between you and their other parent, and react from it within their own bodies. They may take on some of the more toxic energies as their 'responsibility', especially if they are a Second Wave child. And they will most certainly feel any strained relations between you and the other parent in their own bodies. I have personally witnessed this dynamic with my two sons. There are subconscious dynamics driven by the DNA and ongoing relationship issues that the children respond to by 'siding' with one parent or the other and unconsciously adopting characteristics of the parent with whom they are sympathetic; in other words, they unconsciously activate DNA switches within themselves, choosing which aspect of ancestral DNA to embody. They can feel conflicted within their bodies if you are 'at war' with their other parent, even if they never witness an interaction between you. You can't hide the truth because the children feel it in their bodies due to the DNA and how it vibrates between people with closely aligned DNA.

- Being honest and open with your children is the best policy, especially with a Second Wave child. They already 'know' what you think they don't know. Most of them are very psychically aware and have access to their emotional center which taps into that vast body of knowledge in the subconscious. Help them navigate the truth of the current situation by openly discussing things so they can learn the accuracy of their 'knowing', rather than denying or covering up the truth and leaving them to feel crazy. If you are feeling upset and they ask you whether you are upset, admit the truth while letting them know that it's not their responsibility to 'fix' it.

- Be mindful to remove yourself and your child from the Triangle of Disempowerment, and to disentangle energetically to allow the child room to self-express on their own chunk of land. A helpful tool is to teach the child to be a tree. Trees send roots down into the Earth for nurturing. If your child sends roots around you for nurturing, or if you send roots around your child, you'll end up starving each other trying to get the kind of sustenance that can only be provided by the Earth and Spirit. Another way aspect important to mention is that your self-worth is not dependent on your child, and your child's self-worth is not dependent on you.

- If you are annoyed by your child, it's possible you may have some crust to clean up that is influencing your perceptual filters. I became aware of this within myself when I remarried and became a step mother to two young children, 7 and 9. I started noticing an annoyance within myself whenever they would play loudly. A voice in my head would say "Damn kids." That voice was probably always there during my own children's younger years, but went unnoticed in the cacophony of my unconscious mind. It was the voice of my first step father who was a violent drunk, and would punish my mother with a beating if I acted in a way that annoyed him. In other words, if I behaved like a child, my mom would get beat. That's some crust that I needed to remove to fully be present and loving to my children. Awareness of your annoyances, and investigation into the underlying subconscious structures generating the feelings, is essential for being a conscious parent.

- There's more to things than meet the eye. If your child all of a sudden begins acting differently, it may just be growth or it may be something else. Has someone died recently that was close to the child? Expand outside the box of normal thinking to reveal a solution.

♥

Protected By Egoic Structures

The more trauma you experienced as a child, the thicker the crust that gets formed around your Divine Spark as a means of protection from the Personality or egoic self. Often we can feel like the ego is our enemy, but actually it has been the protector of the pure essence that came down into a physical body. I love the story that GP Walsh shared on Soul Nectar Show to help us understand this point. He painted the picture of the President of the United States in the limo with the big procession of cars and security on the way to the White House. All eyes are on this procession, but the President in the limo is actually a decoy. The real President is entering the back of the White House in an unmarked car. This is the same for us humans. The egoic or Personality Self is the one in the limo getting all the attention, while the soul essence is going in through the back door unwitnessed and unassuming. In this way we can be grateful to our Personality Self for being the decoy and taking all the difficult hits in our lifetime.

But now that the soul is ready to command the ship, we need to understand how to dismantle the Personality protection system to allow the soul to lead. And that part can be a bit tricky, as I'm sure you've become aware. The Personality or egoic Self can be very slippery. As you begin transforming and reducing its power, the Personality becomes even more slippery in an effort to go undetected by your Awareness. The key is to make the Personality your ally, so it does not feel threatened into hiding deep in your shadows. Give the Personality a new role as you transition its former responsibilities to your soul. So that's tip #1: Make the Personality your ally and give it an important role so it can let go of control and let your soul lead the way.

A helpful pathway for understanding the resistance of the Personality is the concept introduced by Jett Psaris in *Undefended Love* of the cracked identity and the compensatory identity. The cracked identity holds the core wounds from childhood and the beliefs that cripple all of us: not good enough, unwanted, unseen, unheard, unworthy, and so forth. The cracked identity within is a painful place where we store the wounds we did not know how to handle as a child. The compensatory identity is a persona we build in life to counter all the wounds of the cracked identity. You can think of it like a layer that covers up the wounds with messages directly contradicting the wounded beliefs under the surface.

For example, you may have a core wounded belief in your cracked identity that you're not good enough, and so over time you create this compensatory identity as a person who is perfect in appearance. You say the right things, you do really well in school, you have wonderful manners so you attract a lot of friends. But underneath, no matter how many accomplishments in life you claim for yourself, you never really feel good enough. This is because the cracked identity is underneath the surface of your polished life reminding you all the time that you're an imposter.

Tip #2: Make spaciousness to notice those inner farts as they arise because those are precious messages from your cracked identity surfacing for your awareness. Explore those and heal another layer of the cracked identity. As you heal the core wounds of the cracked identity, you remove the need for the compensatory identity and it can relax its efforts to protect you from the 'ugly truth' that it fears will send you into a tailspin. As the compensatory identity relaxes, you can step into greater authenticity as your true self and the need for both of these false Personality constructs diminishes in your consciousness.

Another helpful system for understanding the mechanics of the false Personality is the book from Jose Stevens called *Transforming Your*

Dragons: How to Turn Fear Patterns into Personal Power. In this book, Jose reveals the core 'dragons' that challenge every human to recoil back into the Personality Self. Once you understand the dragons and how they got a hook in you from childhood, you can start untangling the strategies that have, up until now, kept these defenses in place. The seven dragons are greed, self-deprecation, arrogance, impatience, martyrdom, self-destruction, and just plain stubbornness. Exploring this topic can be extremely triggering, and that is a good sign that you are discovering within yourself the existence of these egoic structures.

Tip #3: Dismantle the power of these dragons in your life by reading this book and doing the exercises. Open to explore how these dragons have sneaked their way into your consciousness, and decide to do the suggested work to liberate yourself from them. This book offers very powerful insights into the egoic structures that keep you in Personality and out of soul presence.

Most of what has been suggested in this section so far is incredibly triggering. Wonderful! The triggering helps you become aware of what has been hidden in the shadows. Now let's discuss a soothing remedy after all that triggering: child healing. Typically the ways our Personality protects us stem from patterns that began in childhood, before we were cognitively capable of reasoning and discerning. When I work with clients and students, we use the triggering explorations suggested in this section to uncover the 'inner farts' that usually hide out in our shadows. Then we apply healing techniques to release the old energy and transform consciousness with new patterns.

One of the methods I use is childhood healing in which the client tunes into the feeling of the 'inner fart' and then invites into an imaginal healing space the Inner Child who first felt this way. We then work with the Inner Child to resolve the misunderstanding, clear up the old energy, and insert a new productive pattern. Working at the energetic and imaginal spaces transforms consciousness very quickly, and then through concerted effort the client can bring the new patterns to the material through action in her life.

And so Tip #4: Explore the 'inner farts' to reveal the core wound of the Inner Child and heal it.

♥

Past Lives, Imprints and Walk Ins

Part of what we are clearing as part of the Second Wave is karma from past lives. Ancestral karma passed down to us through our DNA, as well as personal karma earned in other lifetimes on Earth. Karma is simply an imbalance in the energy caused by leaning too far in one polarity or other, and having to bring the energy back into right relationship by experiencing the other side of the coin, so to speak. If you steal from someone, then karma is to have someone steal from you, or perhaps to witness someone you love being stolen from, so you can see what it feels like to have something stolen.

When we live a life disconnected and asleep, it's possible to perpetrate a number of 'sins' that then must be rectified. If we do not correct an imbalance during a lifetime, the karma is stored until a later lifetime when we pre-arrange situations with other souls that allow us to experience what we must to restore right relationship. At least, this is how Earth has been operating for thousands of years.

During this time of the Second Wave, the Akashic Records have been restored and healing modalities made available to help humanity to clean up the karmic debt. So naturally as a participant in the Second Wave, you will likely have encountered a modality to help clear your karma. For souls who have had many lifetimes on Earth, this karma is naturally from past lives, and using modalities like past life regression or Quantum Healing Hypnosis Technique, you may remember other lifetimes and the situations that led to the creation of the karma you are now working to clear in this lifetime.

If you are a volunteer from somewhere else in the galaxy, the past lives you 'remember' might be more like allegories designed to tell you a story that helps you resolve a current challenge on your path. Or what you 'remember' might be a memory accessed from the collective consciousness for the benefit of your understanding. Or the past lives you 'remember' might be implants in your field.

Implants are memories of past lives that seem real in the sense that there are visuals, scenes, and even emotions from another lifetime that you assume must belong to your soul. However, there's only a moment that you remember…and there are no other details or memories from that lifetime that surface. The memory lacks depth in this way. It's just a small hologram designed to help you personally experience something so you can draw a lesson from it.

When I first started attempting to access past lives, I went to a past life regression expert and had a very frustrating session. I lay there with absolutely no results. No visions, no knowing…nothing. Later that day I was cycling at the gym and obsessing over this abyss, making plans to contact a better expert to get some results. Suddenly a male voice came into my head and very loudly spoke "You have a life. Live it." I now know that voice was from Archangel Michael, and the directive was given to me primarily because I was avoiding my life task work by looking into past lives. And secondarily because…I didn't have any past lives on Earth to look into. Shortly after this shocking moment, I proceeded down the path that would trash my marriage and lead to a radical 90 degree turn whereby I became a Soul Guide. Moral: You can't skip this life's work by losing yourself in the stories of other lifetimes.

More recently, I have experienced QHHT sessions where I 'remembered' past lives; but then during the experience realized that these remembrances were really more like parables that Spirit was sharing with me for the purpose of helping me to understand some lessons. These 'past lives' have vanished very quickly in their tangibility; once the understanding was complete, the needed healing was done and the memory faded.

What has been most profound is my experience of a Walk In. It took me awhile to understand this experience, years in fact, to the place where I now know that I have a Walk In that resides within me. At least four years before the writing of this book, I was visiting the

Cherokee replica village in the Smoky Mountains with my sons. I had been trying to locate a Cherokee shaman to assist me in making the connection to my ancestry beyond the veil, since making a DNA connection or finding my ancestor on the rolls was not working.

As I asked around the village for help, I was finally led to a man working making flint knives as part of a demonstration. I was brought to tears with my heart-felt request to be connected to my lineage, and this man agreed to meet me after his shift in the parking lot. Feeling hopeful, I turned away from him and started walking down the path to the exit when something extraordinary happened. I felt a ball of energy the size of a softball penetrate the back of my head where my skull meets my neck. I now know that this area is a spiritual gateway called the 'Mouth of God.' I instantly felt dizzy and expansive, and had to sit down. Looking at a tree nearby, I was able to see it breathing. (Seeing the trees breathe lasted several weeks after this moment.)

Following this experience I became aware of what I thought was a past life as a Cherokee medicine man and chief. I felt tremendous grief at the memories that surfaced in my mind. I remembered watching countless women, men and children in my tribe die along the Trail of Tears. If I turned my thoughts to this man during my day, I would often burst into tears with the sadness of it all. I became convinced that I had experienced a spontaneous soul retrieval. My memory and feelings of his life were powerful, and felt like my own. I was still a student of the Four Winds at this time, and was practicing soul retrieval for clients. This was different, but I made the assumption that it must be a different type of soul retrieval.

When I began stepping into my purpose, there were many times that his suffering emerged as something that needed attention and healing in order for me to progress in my business. So I dedicated a great deal of time healing this aspect of self in my training programs and thereafter. I always felt his presence as a quiet observant watcher of my activities, and there were many times that other healers and clairvoyants saw him in my field and received messages from him for me. The primary message from my Cherokee man was "Too many thinking", as he stood arms crossed looking disapproving.

The more I performed healing sessions, I also had clients who would open their eyes mid-session and see him in my face, or standing just behind me. Several psychics told me they saw him move from inside me to behind me and around me, always moving in and out of my field. I knew he was helping me to learn the art of being a healer and working with the allies and ancestors beyond the veil. I welcomed his wisdom in my life to help me become more skilled and wise.

One time I was with a coach on a private retreat near Atlanta, which was Cherokee land in the distant past, and I did a little drum journey. We both felt the presence of hundreds of souls in the night, moving toward us to the sound of the drum. His drum. It was an awe-inspiring moment.

When I worked with plant medicine, I became aware of him when drumming during a ceremony. One ceremony he was in front of me, his long grey hair loose around his face, his wrinkled brown face looking kindly at me. "Let me drum" he said, and I relinquished control, amazed that I did not have to control my right hand as it beat the drum. He did it for me, and I entered a new dimension in the drum beat, relaxing with his support and learning from him.

About a year before publishing this book, I integrated my Cherokee Chief "White Eagle Chief" within my being in a meditation where we made peace between our lineages...white Western woman and brown Medicine Man. We forgave each other, expressed our love of each other, and joined as one consciousness with two aspects. Since this huge healing and 'soul retrieval,' I have become aware that I am not actually of this planet, and that my Cherokee Chief agreed to assist me in this life. His expertise over many lifetimes as a healer and leader on Earth have served me well on my mission to this planet, and I am grateful for his support and wisdom.

Discernment is very important when assessing your personal experience of a past life, imprint, or Walk In. This is why I have invited my friend Lisa Barnett to contribute her wisdom to this section of the book. She offers information from the Keepers of the Akashic Records about these topics to help you navigate your own journey a bit better.

My guides tell me that Walk Ins typically only happen if you require assistance to accomplish your mission. It doesn't happen for everyone. And sometimes what you think is a Walk In could be something else, which is why I've invited Lisa to share her expertise here. I encourage you to explore your own knowing with all of the information provided here to determine how it resonates for you. Your experience is unique, and it's really up to your inner guidance to put the puzzle pieces into place. Of course, if you need help integrating or processing your experience, reach out.

♥

Now I introduce another good friend to share with you some aspects of her wisdom around soul agreements, walk-ins, imprints and karma clearing in the Akashic Records. Lisa Barnett is the internationally recognized bestselling author of *"The Infinite Wisdom of the Akashic Records"* and her newest book *"From Questioning to Knowing – 73 Prayers to Transform Your Life"*.

Lisa Barnett has devoted her life as an Akashic channel to help people connect to their divinity and receive the soul guidance as they are healing and transforming their lives. She is the Founder of Akashic Knowing School of Wisdom where she has spent more than 20 years working with thousands of clients and students around the world to help them to access personal soul wisdom, healing and guidance for life, in their Akashic Records.

Lisa's specialty is empowering individuals to find greater fulfillment, happiness, abundance, health, and ease by helping them align with their soul path, understand their soul contracts, and complete their karma and vows.

Insights from an Akashic Channel by Lisa Barnett

I share with you from the position and view of having been an Akashic Record Keeper myself many millennia ago.

I will share a bit about myself so you can understand how many of us come to know what we know. For me it started with a very unusual realization at the early age of three and that experience has informed most of my life.

At the time, I remember trying to explain something to my mother but being only three, I was lacking in the vocabulary department. I remember looking down at my hands and thinking "I'm trapped in a body"! It was a very scary feeling and I told my mother that I wanted to go back. Of course there was no way for her to send me "home" but that feeling and memory became the impetus to start searching for answer to the big questions that so many of us have. Questions like "Why am I here?" or "Why would I be born into this abusive family?"

I started reading all the spiritual books I could find at fourteen years old and went on to minor in Philosophy in college. No one else that I knew had the memories of being an Etheric soul nor could they answer any of my questions. I read about past lives and reincarnation and eventually became an intuitive energy healer.

That sounds like a smooth path but let me say I spent over fifteen year "off roading" it. I forgot who I was, went into corporate work, spent too much time trying to fit in and be what I thought other humans came to be, until I got really sick and had to stop and figure out what had happened to me. As I healed my illness I found the memories of "before being in a body" and that's when I realized I'd come to be a healer and to share divine wisdom.

After a few years of working with clients there were times when I was doing an intuitive healing session and I would find myself moved to a much vaster place. In this void, I received information about past, present and occasionally the future for my client. I could see the way a person's experience in this life was related to other lifetimes. Sometime it was the gifts and talents they were bringing forward but more often it was their challenges, blocks and illness that were showing up to be understood in a Big Picture sort of way. It took me almost five years of this "hit or miss" type connection before I realized I was speaking to the Keepers of the clients' Akashic Records.

Once I realized I had this gift and the Record Keepers gave me a vibrational key to make it easy and fast to access the Akashic Record, I could fully step into this profound work fulltime. I will share some of what they have taught me over these 20 years and what I've learned from working with 11,000 clients.

One of the important aspects to realize is that you actually have a personal manual. You wrote a Soul Plan before you came into your body this time. In this plan you made soul contracts with soul family members and other souls you've known in past lives or even in other dimensions.

The fact that you've have hundreds of past lives is more important than many people think. You may think, I don't care if I was a king or some famous painter so the past isn't important to me. What I would suggest to you is that it is your past that creates your present. It is from all the various lives that you choose the talents you want to have and share in this life as well as the soul growth lessons you're interested in learning. Your soul's purpose is based on the numerous lives in which you were living your life in alignment to a certain gift and talent.

I think most of us would then believe that we would have wonderful and easy lives if we're the ones in charge of our own soul's plan but we really come to Earth to learn and grow as a soul. That includes challenging and traumatic situations and life circumstances. It is the challenges that offer ways to stretch beyond our comfort zone and allow us to have new realizations. Through trial and error we learn new ways of reacting or creating. An inventor is a great example of someone who learns through trial and error. We, as humans, are inventors of a higher way of being, always moving toward awakening and enlightenment, whether you are conscious of it or not. The process of trying new ways of thinking and even feeling is the way we invent a happier, easy life for ourselves. If we don't change and grow when we're in a negative situation then we stagnate. For an inventor that would mean no new creations and for a soul that would appear as a person stuck in an old pattern, unable to move forward in their life. It would feel like emotional pain, lack, fear and maybe depression or illness and poverty. As rough as it sounds, our souls choose challenges in order to kick us out of our comfort zone and into action.

Imagine that you came together with a soul that you have had many past lives with. You made a soul contract, on the Etheric plane, before embodying. You and this soul wanted to grow by overcoming some challenges you two had experienced together in other lives. In those lives you have had a variety of relationships but they all included what we call "Karma" which means, a challenge or obstacle that gives your souls a chance to learn something new about life so you both can grow your soul's wisdom. If the person/soul was unable to learn the lesson, that means the karma wasn't complete because the lesson wasn't learned so they come back and do it again and again until we complete the karmic puzzle.

Now in your life, that soul is your present life father. You both came to support each other and to share wisdom and love so you could work through challenging patterns which sometimes appear to us as terrible traumas. Once you've written the soul contract and are now in a body, you have what appears as a distressing and painful relationship with your father. Since you came to support and teach about love and wisdom, you find yourself born to an alcoholic. This soul who is now your parent tends toward escaping reality through alcohol, drugs and other addictive behaviors. You both knew this was the soul contract before you embodied, but now that you're here, it sucks.

As a soul, you thought that by loving your father enough he would "remember" who he really is, as a wise, infinite soul, and find a better way to work through his emotional pain on this dense Earth plane than by escaping with alcohol. As you know, that is sometimes the case, a parent will drastically change their lifestyle when they have a child, but that is not always the way it works out. You may care for him, cooking and cleaning and even getting the bills paid. You may wonder why you aren't good enough for him to sober up for you. You may even try to take on his karma, which is not possible, in case you haven't been told that. You may also take on his painful emotions which you now think of yours.

In the end you may end the relationship in frustration and sadness. You held up your side of the soul contract and now it's your father's turn to work through his side of the contract and for you to release the pain that is not even yours and to heal your lack of self love because you think you failed your dad.

Your father may not complete this karma in this life. You may even find yourself in another life, back in a similar relationship, trying to teach that same soul to love more deeply and feel more clearly and to find another way.

The Akashic Record Keepers say that most souls, once they've come into the Earth karmic pattern, it takes hundreds of lifetimes to work through all the mess we create. That could be 500 to 800 lifetimes, repeating patterns and not learning the lessons we've come to learn. The repeating patterns are what most people call karma and the learning and understanding about challenging situations is how you grow as a soul. Karma is never a punishment, it really is how we learn and grow.

The Record Keepers also tell us that the easiest way to clear karma is through forgiveness. When we can forgive the soul, who is also a light being on a journey, you can then move into compassion and love which will release old karma throughout time. Even if you have been struggling with one soul to help them awaken and they continue with their addictive patterns, you can free yourself from the soul contract which has this karma attached to it. When you can love them unconditionally, even if they can't or don't love you back, you free yourself from the pattern of being the savior and it's easier to move forward with your life, knowing that you have done your best and the karmic lesson is theirs to learn. I'm not suggesting you abandon your addictive parents, children or friends but when you give them their karma back, let them learn their lessons in their own time and way, you are able to do your own personal karmic work or possibly share your gifts, love and compassion with people who are willing to receive it and thus complete their own patterns and lessons.

This is the way it's been for hundreds of thousands of years, with our ancient soul writing a soul plan which outlines and creates our life. Based on hundreds of past lives, karmic patterns and our soul's desire to learn and grow, share gifts and talents, and eventually ascend.

At this time in history, things are changing for many people, the Record Keepers are saying. As you may know, there has been a big wave of new types of people coming to Earth. Since the dawning of the Age of Aquarius in the 1960's we've had the Indigos, the Crystal and most recently the Rainbow children. All have come with their unique abilities and their desire to transform the world. Many of them do not fit into the old pattern. Some I've worked with have come to complete all their outstanding karma in this one life and help others to do the same. It does not make for an easy life, but many who are working through the old energy that way are very conscious of it. And the newest of the groups, the Rainbow children, seem to have come without any old karma at all.

Some of these light workers find they are walk-in, with a variety of soul types inhabiting the body now. In case you're not familiar with the term, here is a definition: A walk-in is a new-age concept of a person whose original soul has departed the body and has been replaced with a new, generally more advanced, soul.

Some of the walk-ins are actually embodying the original soul's Over Soul, instead of a new soul, which is the classic definition. This means that all of their extensive soul wisdom and knowledge is coming through into the body now. It may be that some of the sudden awakening experiences that people are having are people being able to completely embody the extensive Over Soul.

Some people I've met are the classic type of walk-in, which means the original person dies, very briefly, and that original soul released their body to another higher vibrational soul to bring new information and wisdom to the world. These new walk-ins may have had a "near death experience" and remember some of the original soul's memories. For many, it's very confusing, until they can integrate more of the truth of who they are as a new soul, coming into an adult body.

Some of these walk-ins have very little Earth experience and so they may have an imprint of Earth memories or they may find they have a "body memory" which comes from the original owner of that body, even though the soul has moved on. This helps the walk-in to function on the Earth plane with greater ease. If you have an "imprint" it would be like watching hundreds of movies about life on Earth throughout history and then feeling and believing that you lived all those lives. You may at some point realize they are imprinted memories and not really your own, but they served you well.

Not all of the Second Wavers are walk-ins. Some may just feel that they don't belong here or fit in. Some feel they have no real connection to anything or anyone. Robert Heinlein coined a great phrase with the title of his book: *Stranger in a Strange Land*. I remember reading that book in 1968 and realizing that that was my truth.

When I read the Akashic Records of these people they are often galactic travelers or from a different planet. They haven't spent many lives here on Earth but do have some experience, maybe only 10 – 25 lifetimes, and they have come to bring new inventions and ideas from other worlds to humanity. Many of these souls, as well as the walk-ins, have no karma. They have never gotten stuck in the karmic loops or patterns that come from hundreds of lifetimes here.

When the Records Keepers asked me to start an Akashic School and teach this empowerment tool, they also told me that I was very galactic. They explained that as ancient souls we travel throughout the galaxies and live in many different realms. They have offered us six vibrational keys, which are access prayers to the Akashic Realm. When you learn to access your Akashic Records with Akashic Knowing school, you also connect with some of your soul's original home planets. By teaching you these access prayers which resonate with a variety of soul lineages, you may receive more information about who you are in the expansive realms and universes as well as learn more about what your soul wants to do here on Earth at this amazing time in history.

♥

Unplugging from the Karmic Collective Consciousness

Everything you see in your reality is by your agreement to it. Your built-in reticular activating system filters the overwhelming amount of information available in your environment to bring to your attention only those awarenesses that serve to reinforce your agreements. In other words, you see what you believe.

When you want to shift your reality, you start by becoming aware of what you have already agreed to that is causing you to experience the conditions in your reality. Then you can make a new choice about those agreements and begin to train your reticular activating system to make you aware of conditions that match your new choices. Curiosity is an ally in this retraining process as it helps to open up your mind to become aware of new possibilities you formerly overlooked.

The agreements that govern your reality from your subconscious are those things this text has already addressed — ancestral karma, early childhood brain training, patterns grooved into your brain by repetition — and, agreements in the collective consciousness (or unconsciousness).

What is the collective consciousness? In a nutshell, the collective consciousness is a co-created reality we engage in, often without realizing we are engaging in it. The collective consciousness has a book of beliefs and rules that are often unspoken, but which people just know. When someone comes into a collective consciousness from the outside, they often unintentionally break these unspoken rules and that disrupts the flow that the collective consciousness expects, resulting in censure. The collective consciousness also has shared memories that help people to be 'in the know' and thereby have a feeling of being connected. There is a strong pull that can be felt inside a human body to be part of the collective consciousness, and to 'fit in.' For people who do not feel accepted by the collective consciousness, there can also be a pull to be a 'rebel' and break out.

For example, in the collective consciousness of the United States, it's generally accepted that you stand a foot or more away from a person when speaking to them. There are funny moments in sitcoms where someone broke this rule and stood too close, being ridiculed as a 'close talker.' The cultural paradigm of watching television sitcoms is brought into office environments to reinforce the cultural norm of not standing too close by monitoring people's behavior and using the code word 'close talker' to identify those breaking the unspoken rule. Most people will avoid standing too close so as to prevent themselves from being labeled by the group as a 'close talker.' A rebel might jokingly play with this social norm by standing too close and then calling attention to it. But they are all agreeing to the same 'rules.'

When you watch mainstream television, movies, and news you become aware of what most of the collective consciousness of the people in the United States are believing and remembering so they can be 'in the know' and part of the group. If you participate in the collective consciousness fully, you'll have the television on in the background of your home, or while you fall asleep, and thereby allow your brain to be programmed subliminally by the messages on the television from advertisement, news, sitcoms, or whatever you're tuned into. When you become conscious about it, and actively pay attention to any of this content, you can have a whole new realization about why you might 'know' that pharmaceuticals are a good thing to put into your mouth, for example. Do you really 'know' that? Or was your brain programmed subliminally by the advertisements on the television that you had droning in the background of your home, and then reinforced by what you saw around you at work and in your family?

Perhaps you were part of the cultural dynamic of being raised by a mother who watched soap operas as a primary form of entertainment. Maybe you were a latch-key kid left to your own devices, and watched this sort of mind-programming, or any host of the violent aggressive programming available now on television and the Internet. Anything you 'tune into' becomes part of what your mind tells you is 'normal behavior', and this is especially true of a childhood mind. What messages do you think a soap opera conveys? From my personal perspective, what it demonstrates is a normalization of vindictive behavior, gossip, manipulation, secrets and lies, and produces a sort of dark gleeful response in the person who consumes it regularly; is this the kind of food you want to feed your brain, or your child's? What about the violence of Internet and television content today? Can you comprehend how that brain 'food' is desensitizing your heart?

If you stop engaging in the ways that mainstream messages are sent out to a collective, and start tuning into nature and inner explorations, and then reengage with the collective, you'll notice that you're out of sync with other people in the collective. Maybe you'll notice you have less fear after not watching television news for a week. Perhaps you'll notice you have less anxiety after a week of listening to meditation music at bed instead of television. Potentially you'll begin questioning what others are simply taking for granted.

As an example, I had regularly seen the latest mainstream movie for years. Then I became very absorbed in my purpose work and did not go to see a mainstream movie for six months. I chose a movie that was akin to one I would have seen before. I was shocked and dismayed by the gore and violence of this PG13 movie, and even more perplexed why everyone looked un-phased by it as I scanned the audience. It was normal for them. The frog in boiling water syndrome had occurred during my movie sabbatical...no one seemed to know just how much hotter the water was boiling!

Any community to which you tune in has a collective consciousness. New York City has a collective consciousness. Unity Church has a collective consciousness. Your family has a collective consciousness. The class you sign up for at college has a collective consciousness. The Facebook group you join has a collective consciousness.

It's actually a very cool thing to know that each group of humans with which you engage has its own collective consciousness. What you are invited to do is stay awake and aware as you engage with a collective consciousness, and to run everything you notice through your own truth filter with the Divine. This is especially important as you engage with the more mainstream bubbles of consciousness. Just like your physical body is surrounded by a bubble of energy called an aura, a group of people engaging together is also surrounded by a bubble of energy that is the collective consciousness of the group. You are 'connected' to the bubbles of consciousness where you frequently engage, and therefore psychically more aware of the thoughts and experiences of those people within the group. I've learned to be intentional about this as an instructor by creating a specific container for each class, and inviting each student into the container. At the end of the class, we release the container.

As a leader of light, it's helpful to become aware of the collective consciousness bubbles with which you engage. This helps you to identify whether your life experience is being influenced or negatively impacted by a certain collective consciousness bubbles. It also helps you be aware of whether your participation in a particular collective consciousness bubble is unconsciously influencing your opinion on a subject, while your personal truth might be very different.

The awareness about collective consciousness bubbles is an important part of turning upside-down world right-side up. By consciously making new choices aligned with your higher self, you can begin to influence the unconscious patterning of the collective consciousness bubbles with which you engage. Aligning yourself to your inner truth will challenge your fears of being different and cast out of the collective consciousness bubbles with which you engage. As you move through your fear to align to your truth, you energetically disentangle from the unconscious aspects of a collective consciousness bubble, disrupt the unconscious patterns, and begin to influence a change in course for others with whom you're connected.

There are forces that are quite happy with the status quo of collective consciousness bubbles. Family structures are a perfect example. There are entities that have farmed entire family lines for their 'food' which is generally emotional energy such as fear, anger, frustration, rage, and so forth. Without 5th dimensional awareness into the patterns and dynamics of the family collective consciousness, you might accept the notion that a child inherited an anger pattern from the parent. A more accurate statement might be that the child inherited an entity that feeds on the family line, and found a way into the child through fear and the unawareness of the parent to the dynamic. When you energetically remove the entity, the anger issue miraculously clears and becomes a normal matter of self-mastery with feelings. You might need some support from someone with excellent 5th dimensional awareness to see and remove this type of entanglement. A family liberated from parasitic pressures to behave in low-vibrational ways can now make progress on self-mastery initiatives to elevate into higher consciousness.

As you disentangle from unproductive collective consciousness agreements and structures, you may find yourself periodically experiencing a fear response or depression or suicidal ideation. It's best to consult someone with professional experience guiding others in spiritual awakening in these situations. However, from my personal perspective I can share that I do not believe anything is 'wrong.' Often when dense energies are released from our being, they rise and expand within us a very unpleasant difficult feeling that must keep expanding and rising until it dissipates. These inner negativity fogs often have painful words associated with them from repressed negative self-talk. It's also possible that if you're breaking free from an entity attachment, that you'll 'hear' lots of fearful thoughts and feel scared. Ground, shield, clear your energy and soothe yourself with self-compassion as you allow this inner fog to dissipate. Get an awake friend to hold space for you as you face it. What you're experiencing is an old story or old repressed energy that wants to be witnessed as it's released. It's on its way **out**. Give yourself all the support you need to hang tough during the process. Your brain can go a little haywire during these moments; it's best to take no action being suggested by a brain under siege unless it's to call for support. Even the most intense feelings will pass in just a few minutes if you allow them to expand and dissipate with adding fuel to the fire. Once again, if you are experiencing these challenging moments, please reach out to a professional to help guide you through it to the other side.

As you unplug from the karmic or misaligned aspects of collective consciousness, you will become even more aware of how these collective consciousness structures are unconsciously serving to cause injustice or suffering. You'll see more and more of the shadow side. As you become aware of these collective agreements that you no longer wish to be a party to, realign yourself to your inner truth and make new choices to align your life to a new frequency. Rather than focusing on what's wrong out there, forge the bridge to the new reality in your own life and serve as an example for others. Where we place our attention grows. Without ignoring aspects of collective consciousness that require a new action from you, do your best to expand your attention and energy in the new directions you're choosing to take. Learn how to be **in** the world, but not **of** the world.

Start to forge new collective consciousness bubbles with other awake souls as you are connected to them, and use these alliances to set new elevated intentions for Earth and your personal evolution. The content on your social media feed is an excellent gauge of your current participation in collective consciousness bubbles, and the way it changes as you evolve will reflect back to you this evolution.

♥

Monkey Mind to Mystic

Living in a 3-D world, we start to expect everything to show up as solid, 'real' and grounded as the table and chairs in order to believe it's true. But listening for guidance and messages from the higher dimensions is more subtle. You have to get quiet to hear it, close your eyes to see it, and eliminate external distractions to feel it. The message is probably not going to whack you upside the head…at first.

Monkey mind will keep you from hearing the messages you're meant to hear and act upon for your purpose. The chattering ego is a product of your 3-D world, and until it's realigned to its rightful position in your consciousness, it will produce a lot of mind chatter and distraction to keep you from getting quiet. Collectively, humanity is on the verge of a huge leap in consciousness. So of course, the daily life of the mainstream person is so busy there's barely time to go to the bathroom or drink a glass of water between meetings. The deluge of content to digest is overwhelming, and so people are skimming along the surface of it all trying to keep up. This is exactly where the ego wants you to prevent your awakening.

You've got to make space for daily meditation so you can tune out the exterior, and tune into the ephemeral space of Spirit where all the truly important messages are received. Some lightworkers rely on the external environment to deliver synchronicity and messages via other people, and that's one way to go about it. But when you make space for tuning into your own Great Spirit channel, you can receive clearer guidance way faster and more reliably than hoping it shows up through your environment or consulting someone you think is more psychic. No one has the ability to hear your channel more clearly than you.

If you find it difficult to reach a quiet inner space, your nervous system may need rebalancing out of fight or flight. Shamanic drum journey music is helpful because the pace of its beat is designed to bring your brain out of beta state into alpha and theta where the doorway to the Great Spirit is opened. Breathwork is helpful as well for calming the nervous system; three deep breaths, each one expanding the belly and then releasing, should help you let go of tension. Opening sacred space is helpful because you create a container of protection all around you and solicit help from the Four Directions, Earth allies, and Spirit guides to help you quiet your inner realm to receive guidance. Autonomic writing is helpful as a tool for accessing your soul wisdom as well; you can write a question in your journal, and then allow your hand to just start writing the response without controlling the flow of information. That's essentially how I have written most of this book; it's just that I've used a computer instead of a pen.

Try to focus on simply being available for messages to come through, then receive the messages and capture them accurately. Later you can review and process and see what you make of them. Curiosity is a good focus because it gets the inner judge out of the way; being concerned about getting the 'right' answer will definitely add stress to your mystic ventures.

What I've found is that the messages I receive are confirmed at a later point through some kind of synchronicity. Perhaps another clairvoyant shares the same message with me that I got during my meditation. Maybe I have an animal guide visitation, and when I look up the meaning of the animal guide, I receive confirmation. You can ask your guides to bring you confirmation of messages in a way that you will know their accuracy. I often refine my understanding of insights from meditations by asking questions and using my pendulum over my mesa to retrieve the answers, allowing my stone allies to help me gain greater clarity.

Ultimately, you've got to test your intuitive insights well enough that you arrive at the point of trusting and verifying them. You're not going to get a game plan mailed to you by the Great Spirit, so you must be able to work out a method of internal discernment for taking steps towards your purpose.

And here's often the most challenging part: when you get the clear insight, ACT. We must bring the vision down from the etheric realms to the physical realms by taking action. It's through inspired action that we manifest our purpose. The dreaming space of the upper dimensions is essential to clarifying the vision, and taking inspired action is essential to anchoring the vision in the 3rd dimension.

Don't wait for someone else to validate your vision. If you have clear insight, a knowing in your heart, and inspired actions for your plan: do it. As you take the inspired actions, the pathway unfolds and the next inspired actions are revealed. In this way, the mystical insights become the new reality. Each of us taking our own inspired actions helps us collectively to manifest the New Earth we are co-dreaming in the collective consciousness.

We are on the verge of a new frontier of consciousness on Earth. Every explorer feels the double-edge of excitement and fear. Focus on the excitement.

♥

Urgency, Confusion, Control, Distraction, Resistance, and Initiation

You feel the urgency to do your purpose and start taking action in a big way, and yet you feel confused, distracted, scared, unworthy, ill-prepared, under-funded, and on the edge of hopeless about it. You have gotten visions and messages about your purpose, but doubt them as soon as you consider how to put it into action. Are we really doing this?

Yes. We are doing it. Now.

There's a number of things that could be getting in the way of acting on your purpose. See if any of these resonate.

- Crazy. You may be blocked by the feeling that you're crazy for actually taking action to bring into reality the visions you've been having. Consider the effect of the Karmic Collective Consciousness on your idea of what is 'sane' and what is 'crazy.' In the current upside-down world, what you're being called to create may indeed sound crazy to those around you who are invested in the current paradigm. But we are not staying in the current paradigm, are we? You already know that we are shifting into a New Earth where what you are taking action to bring into manifestation will make PERFECT SENSE. You have to hold the vision of New Earth and be the bridge to it by manifesting your purpose project right here and now. You'll only be called crazy for a short time (which might be the rest of this lifetime, depending on how long it takes us to manifest the shift into New Earth consciousness).

- Control. The paradigm of control may have infected your consciousness and brought its friends—judgement, punishment, and rebellion—with it. You can't manifest your purpose from a control consciousness. You are invited to manifest from an inspiration consciousness that brings the allies of curiosity, learning, and expansion with it. Become curious as you take the steps shown to you by your higher guidance. Where are the steps leading you? What will be the result of each step? How will each step gift you something you need for the ultimate manifestation of your purpose? Also gift yourself compassion for the learning process. You've never done this before; you're learning as you go, just like a toddler learning how to walk. Heck! We are all learning together how to turn this Titanic around and raise it up! Give yourself some grace and space to evolve into the leader you are meant to be.

- Distraction. You know what you need to do, but you avoid doing it by distracting yourself with other (more comfortable and familiar) things that keep you in the existing paradigm. Questions to ask yourself include: Am I afraid of failing? Am I afraid of being seen as a leader? Am I afraid of people knowing I'm weird/different/gifted? Am I afraid of becoming someone people expect to have all the answers, and then not knowing what to say or do? Am I afraid of finding out I actually am crazy? Become aware of when you are distracting from taking action towards your purpose work, and then delve deeper within to reveal the underlying fear that is motivating the distraction. Take some deep breaths with hand over belly and heart to comfort your human aspect, and recommit to taking even one small action right now. Realize you're pushing through the fear membrane of the Karmic Collective Consciousness with each step you take. Celebrate every step you take towards your purpose with a lot of heart-felt appreciation for the forces within aligning to enable this accomplishment! Put yourself into intentional community of other Second Wave volunteers to gift yourself support from other people who 'get it.' Invite support from your multidimensional allies beyond the veil by opening sacred space at the start of every day; refer to the free Opening Sacred Space meditation for help in creating your own practice. Create a sense of play to make it fun to accomplish tasks towards your purpose; for example, make a deck of index cards with a task written on each one, shuffle, and then draw the next task you're going to perform....like purpose work Tarot cards!

- Resistance. Every time you find yourself in resistance that is showing up as negative self-talk, distraction, lack of resources, 'failures,' and so forth...realize you are actually moving through another layer of the fear membrane into an opening where you will enjoy greater power and traction with your purpose.

Another way of looking at it is the visual of the mud-caked glass with the water pouring in. The mud caked at the bottom of the glass is the crust and sludge of old conditions and patterns that used to work for you but will not apply to your new reality. The water you pour in is all of your self-development input, positive vibes, and steps towards purpose. Each time you pour in a healthy dose of new water, some caked mud gets dislodged from the bottom of the glass and glug, glug, glugs its way up your being to be released in the overflow out the top of the glass. In other words, when you feel saturated by the shit, it's on its way out; and the vacuum created by releasing the old makes way for you to receive the new expansion. Stay the course and do not be deterred. Keep re-aligning to your purpose in each moment, allowing your heart to tap into infinite wisdom that guides your way.

- Initiation. When you find yourself confronted by a lot of fear-based situations all at once, it's an initiation into greater capacity, capability, power, prosperity, love, joy, fulfillment, leadership, and so forth. Rise to the challenge and become the leader who claims the purpose you know you are here to fulfill. The visions and inspirations you have received would not have been sent to you unless they are totally true. The Great Spirit is not a tease. At the same time, it's not all going to be handed to you. You've got to grow **into** it through intention, alignment, action, and embodiment. Fear is an illusion; it's the nightmare you have right before you wake up in your lover's arms. Upon waking, you realize you were safe the whole time. Move yourself through the fear to cross the threshold of your next awakening. When you encounter a challenge or roadblock, see it as the Great Spirit showing you where you can cultivate new muscles or greater capacity through the process of overcoming that challenge.

♥

Soul Agreements

For mutual growth and benefit of souls incarnating on Earth, each soul makes agreements with other souls to perform various roles that facilitate learning. For example, you were born to a mother and father to facilitate them learning how to be a parent to you, and to facilitate you learning lessons through inheriting their DNA and experiencing childhood through their family container.

In the human sense, you also make agreements with other people based on inherited conditioning. For example, in your family system, it might be a rule that as the child to your parent, you agree to take responsibility for elder care of your aging parent. As a parent to your own child, you may agree to pay for your child's education. There are innumerable unspoken rules of engagement for your relationships with partner, family and friends that you inherited through childhood conditioning and experiences throughout your life that prompted you to make choices for yourself.

Sometimes the expected conditioned human agreements conflict with the soul-level agreements. In this case, however hard it may be to break from expectations of family and friends, the soul-level agreements supersede the human rules.

For example, let's say you have a family expectation that you will provide housing for your aging parent. However, your soul has called you to be a vagabond for a year and travel the world surfing couches. You will likely feel very confused and unable to move forward because of the conflict between head and heart. If you travel upwards to the 5th dimension or higher, you may receive insight that clears up the mess. What if at a soul level you made the agreement with your parent's soul that you would not be able to fulfill your family expectation so that your parent's Personality would get the opportunity to experience all the fear of being left behind and thereby grow from it into a deeper understanding of the support of the Great Spirit? Withstanding your family's judgment of your soul-led decision will certainly be challenging, and this is your soul's desire to learn to express itself and its knowing no matter what.

One example of soul agreement from my own life concerns my step Dad. He came into my life when I was 5 years old after I had experienced childhood trauma with my natural father and first step-father. He came into my mother's life to support her in learning to become a compassionate parent. A couple of years ago when I was ready to embark on my soul mission, he suddenly died. I remember the morning before he passed I was on my way to Santa Fe for a training to be a healer with the PowerPath. I had spent the night in Lubbock, Texas and rose the next morning to a call with a prospective client that fell through. As I sat in the car before my journey, I decided to spend a few moments meditating.

My inner dialog got very quiet and I felt extremely etheric and expanded in my awareness. I was contemplating my feeling of readiness for the next part of my soul mission, and my frustration at feeling its slow progress in the world. Breathing and steadying myself, I expanded into a deeper quiet. It was then that I heard voices far above my head in the etheric spaces. "She's not ready."

"I am ready!" I retorted in my mind. I heard the voices shifting around and then I came out of my meditation feeling like things had been resolved in my favor. I took off driving the rest of the way to Santa Fe, picked up a girlfriend at the airport, and took a pivotal call with a radio show host who had a million plus followers. Things were really looking up for me!

And then I saw I had a missed call from my mother. When I returned the call I learned that my step Dad, my revered advisor for most of my life, was in the hospital with only one quarter of one lung functional. I dropped off my friend with the group, and turned around to drive 15 hours home to the hospital overnight across dark remote Texas highways. I prayed that the deer and wild hogs stayed off the road as I sped home for one last chance to see my Dad.

I arrived at the hospital at 4am and rested by his bedside for over two hours during which I experienced the most incredible collaborative psychic dream. My Dad guided me to remember shared moments from our lives over those hours. Every time I felt him pull away his consciousness, I beckoned him back to show me more. It was one of the most profound experiences of my life. The next day, he passed away like a big wave of sparkles. He was happy and fulfilled at his death. He was ready to be free of his physical existence.

At some point, I put things together and realized that my Dad made an agreement with me at the soul level to guide me in my physical life up until I was ready to do my soul mission. Then he would guide me from the etheric realms where he would be much more able to assist me in the moment-by-moment nuances of the work. Although I am sad to not have my Dad around, and I miss his laughter and hugging him, I know he is with me more now than he ever was able to be when he was in a body.

The invitation is to look at your relationships in a whole new way: through the lens of soul agreement.

❤

Become Sovereign

When you become sovereign, you claim supreme authority over yourself. Only from sovereignty are you free of the human drama because you no longer 'need' anything from outside of you for your happiness. This doesn't mean that you are an island all to yourself. This means that you are not dependent on another person for money, safety, love, self-worth or self-identity. A sovereign person follows her own path without needing validation from anyone outside of herself. A sovereign person accesses higher guidance within himself to chart the course of his life.

The road to sovereignty most definitely is benefitted by mentorship from others who have Walked the Beauty Way and claimed sovereignty for themselves. Such a mentor will not presume to know your answer, but can certainly help you become aware of egoic traps, and learn to navigate your own inner guidance system.

A significant part of the journey to sovereignty is releasing everyone in your life from obligation to you. Anything you have expectation that a certain person will say or do for you, or give you, is a way that you get ensnared by the human drama. Anything you judge about another person and hold resentment about is surely entangling you in karma with that other person.

There are several powerful hooks that draw you back into the human drama and cause you to dim your light: expecting money from a particular source, deriving self-worth from power or status, putting people in hierarchies of worth/status, feeling lack or scarcity, thinking you're special or different or more spiritual, needing validation from outside of yourself, needing love from specific people, and letting other people tell you who you are (good or bad).

The goal of personal sovereignty is to fully self-validate, love yourself completely, and follow your inner guidance system—even if doing so causes key individuals in your life (such as your mother or father or partner) to challenge your worth, withhold love or money, or resort to lower vibration human dramas such as bullying.

Watch the hooks from your family system that are designed to suck you back into the family drama. If family drama unfolds, see it as the behavior of people tangled up in the karmic collective consciousness and release yourself from the karma. Every time you find a hook that causes you suffering, do your personal work to release yourself from the expectation that hooked you back into the drama.

Liberating yourself is a painful process, and completely worth it.

♥

Suggestions

Bow To Your Ancestors The Releasing Bow practice comes from Gary Stuart of "Ancestral Intelligence". Think of the ancestral pattern or energy that you no longer wish to carry forward into your life that you know comes from your ancestry. You desire to create a boundary with that pattern or energy so it remains in the past with your ancestry and does not carry forward into your future.

This process involves expressing what you want to let go of, bowing to your ancestors with honor and respect, leaving the burden of the past with your ancestors, turning 180 degrees to face your future and walking forward.

You can find a full procedure for The Releasing Bow at https://garystuarthealing.com/2018/04/bow-card/

Reclaim Past Life Wisdom You are a wise and ancient person with hundreds of lifetimes filled with amazing experiences. You have been or done most things imaginable. However, we often feel so small and incapable. It is the game our soul plays. We wish to remember the truth of who we are. Wise and ancient souls who are able to create and manifest our desires.

Lisa Barnett has created a meditation to help you remember and reclaim this wisdom so you can move forward feeling supported and secure in creating exactly what your heart desires.

Claim it here: https://akashicknowing.com/reclaim-past-life-wisdom-meditation/

Quotes

"We are not meant to stay wounded. We are supposed to move through our tragedies and challenges and to help each other move through the many painful episodes of our lives. By remaining stuck in the power of our wounds, we block our own transformation. We overlook the greater gifts inherent in our wounds—the strength to overcome them and the lessons that we are meant to receive through them. Wounds are the means through which we enter the hearts of other people. They are meant to teach us to become compassionate and wise." — Caroline Myss

"Tell everyone you know: 'My happiness depends on me, so you're off the hook.' And then demonstrate it. Be happy, no matter what they're doing. Practice feeling good, no matter what. And before you know it, you will not give anyone else responsibility for the way you feel—and then, you'll love them all. Because the only reason you don't love them, is because you're using them as your excuse to not feel good." — Esther Hicks

"Life will give you whatever experience is most helpful for the evolution of your soul. How do you know this is the experience you need? Because it's the one you are having."
— Eckhart Tolle

"Truth is a pathless land, and you cannot approach it by any path whatsoever, by any religion, by any sect ... You have to be your own teacher and your own disciple. You have to question everything that man has accepted as valuable, as necessary." — Jiddu Krishnamurti

"Come out of the masses. Stand alone like a lion and live your life according to your own light." — Rajneesh

How You Can Bridge To New Earth

One of my biggest fears with putting this message out in to the world was being called crazy, being mocked, and being discredited by other people. Do you have similar fears? What the Great Spirit helped me to realize through a powerful sound healing experience is that the majority of humans have a very thick crust. This crust prevents the refinement of perception that would allow them to connect with and understand the content of this book. As we raise up consciousness overall on the planet, the layers of crust for humans will begin to melt or dissolve, making it possible for more people to 'get it.' The use of certain plant medicines will also help remove crust and refine perceptual filters to allow people to become more aware.

In the meantime, it's best for those self-identifying as the Second Wave to courageously continue to bring your messages out into the world. See contrary responses as a product of ignorance from a sleepy human who does not yet understand the gift they are turning away. Send blessings and keep moving and sharing to wake up those who are at a level of refinement with their perception to be able to receive this information. Don't take it personally if humans thick in the crust react poorly to your message. As Jesus advised, "Father, forgive them, for they know not what they do" (Luke 23:34). Be in your discernment to know the level of understanding of the people you interact with, but let go of any judgements that arise within you and send love. From Paul Selig's work, "I am Love through the one I see before me."

Another fear you might have is the fear of drowning in other people's needs as you step out into the world and share your gifts and capabilities. Keep very clear boundaries around your gifts and purpose in the world. We are not here to rescue others from their soul agreements and Earth school curriculum. We are simply here to help them awaken to tools, perspectives and practices that help them navigate their incarnation a bit better.

Be mindful of any places where you step into super hero, and ask yourself "How does it feed my egoic self to be a rescuer?" You do not need to be Atlas shouldering the world through the darkness. You are only invited to be an alarm clock to wake up the sleepy humans around you. From time to time the angel lifts a person out of the depths to a new vantage point. As healers, we also offer this gift from time to time. But if it becomes a regular thing for you, you may want to take a closer look to reveal the motivating factors. Clear boundaries are a very good ally for the work of the Second Wave.

Don't be tossed about at the surface of the water where the storm is happening. Don't believe the fear. Claim spaciousness and the deep ocean. Be the particle that invites the wave. Be the voice in the middle of the egoic world that invites the spaciousness and grace of the Great Spirit. Open sacred space over conversations, meetings, organizations, companies, your family, and so forth. Bring the Great Spirit into your world to help yourself and others to break free from the constant **doing** and busyness and attempts by the ego to stay in control by creating so much doing and particles and things that there's not **space** for the Great Spirit. In this way, **be** the demonstration of having one foot in the secular and the other in the spiritual: integrating two worlds through your own vessel.

Look for ways to be a bridge builder for others to Walk the Beauty Way. What words resonate with the people around you? How can you demonstrate a soul-led life in a way that inspires others? Become aware of your surroundings and listen to the words and beliefs of the people to discover the messages that will awaken them to a new level of understanding. If appropriate, steer conversations in a new direction from a loving space within you, rather than from judgement and repulsion. Keep elevating your frequency with continued self-mastery by Walking the Beauty Way yourself and then resonate your upgraded consciousness everywhere you go. Remember that you are always emitting photon packages of light with the ascension codes you have embodied to everyone you meet. Sometimes building a bridge doesn't need words: it just needs you to show up fully present with your big bright light.

Let yourself be in process.[9] You don't have to be perfect. If you were perfect, you would be an ascended master on the other side of the veil helping all of us down here on Earth. No one on this Earthly plane is 'perfect.' We are all in the midst of an infinite evolutionary cycle, learning and co-creating together as we make new inner and outer discoveries.

Let yourself put particularly sticky things on pause and percolate. Breathe into it and invite spaciousness. Allow it to unfold. Stop forcing life to arrive at a certain destination before you love yourself. Start now.

Everything that came before has brought you to where you stand today and so it was all perfect. It was part of your cosmic dance with the Great Spirit. Stop judging it and shaming it. Become curious about why it all happened and what gifts you received from every challenging moment up until now. Bring yourself to feel grateful for it. All of it. Don't force that either. Just welcome the exploration of why you might be grateful for all that happened, and let the Great Spirit whisper to your heart.

As you welcome the Great Spirit to a personal conversation, you unlock the gifts lying dormant in your heart. You're the only one who can claim these gifts.

As you claim the gifts in your heart, you begin to love yourself. Truly, deeply, love yourself. You begin to radiate love in your energy field, and your eyes begin to sparkle...which people start to notice.

Your access to your self-love and soul connection wakes up people around you just by being an expression of your essential self in the world.

You attract people's attention and they start watching you, to see why you're glowing. True sparkle and glow has the resonance of the Great Spirit and it beckons them to their own sparkle and glow. And this is where your self-mastery becomes the demonstration by which others learn to bridge to their own souls.

This is how we bridge to New Earth. By loving ourselves and shining. By Walking the Beauty Way and practicing self-mastery in every moment. By being in process and learning how to embody love, forgiveness, and compassion in response to whatever is arising. By listening to the Great Spirit, sharing the messages, and courageously taking the inspired actions…even if we only see one step ahead. You only need to know the next step to lead the way.

♥

Know Your Own Truth

The most important work you can be doing is to know your own truth. This is a process of aligning to your true vibration and listening to your own station. When you are standing in your own truth, your field resonates with that truth which attracts to you those you are meant to serve. In other words, being the vibration of your own truth is more important than any marketing you might do to promote your services (if you are called to share your gifts as a service business).

While the words you speak about yourself are important to convey information to others, the more powerful force for creating understanding is **being** your truth. The resonance of your truth pulsating from your energy field communicates much more powerfully than content generated from your thinking mind.

To increase the percentage of your being that is resonating at your highest truth, you must navigate the inner workings of your consciousness to identify those aspects of self that are frozen in history and bring them up to date. This is unhooking yourself from the past that echoes through your mind, or has been stored unprocessed in your cells. Historical resonance detracts from the power of your essential-self resonance, causing dissonance in your field that confuses you and those you meet as to who you are in truth.

The subconscious work of unhooking yourself from historical resonances involves a lot of inner listening, and identifying the source of the various 'voices' you hear within.

First you must make the decision to listen within, which means to become aware of the repeating voices or echoes and linger there. Normally we ignore or push aside the echoing voice because we've heard it so many times and we don't want to 'go there' with it again. For this process, you want to capture all these echoes as they arise in your consciousness because they hold a key to fulfilling your purpose in this incarnation.

Make a list of these echoing voices and repeating messages.

Then invest some time to explore each of these repeating messages. One helpful tool is to do a Child Healing Meditation in which you invite the child who created this repeating message to come forward for inquiry and healing; I do this process with my clients and students. Shifting just one message from the past unlocks a great deal of future potential, so this is solid gold for your growth.

A tool you can try for yourself is autonomic writing. My friend Debbie Lynn Grace shared her version of this tool with me which is to take a piece of paper and invite a conversation with the aspect of self who is repeating the message in your mind. You can ask it questions just as you would in a conversation face-to-face, and then hand over the pen to allow that aspect of self to respond. Do it spontaneously without thinking, and you will experience a message from a part of your consciousness that has been ignored up until now.

Now it's your job to coach that aspect of self into a different point of view or a more productive role that aligns with your goals. Offer that aspect something helpful to do in exchange for releasing the historical message to the past. Notice how things unfold differently in your mind as relates to that recurring voice...maybe you notice you don't hear it as often, or it's easier to shift whenever it arises.

Another tool is recapitulation which is accessing that earlier part of you where the story or message was imprinted, releasing the un-expressed feelings about the event, reclaiming any energy lost during the event, and then visualizing a different outcome for that event from the past. Recapitulation is an ancient Toltec practice that includes breathwork combined with meditative visualization.

Along this process of inner inquiry you may discover child selves, recreated versions of your parents, energy that belongs to other people that you took on, past life energy, and so forth. It's important to identify and name the voice that speaks a certain recurring message so you know the appropriate way to handle it. If it is a child self, you can give it a new role. If it is a wounded voice, you can offer it nurturing and redirection. If it is energy that does not belong to you, but is causing disruption in your field, you can command it out of your field and return it from whence it came. This is particularly important if you have a parent who is holding disruptive energy around your evolution; you want to set a good boundary and release any energy you may be holding historically from that person. Your parents and grandparents have influence over your DNA because their consciousness can vibrate their thoughts at a DNA level in your body; so set good boundaries. You don't really need to know what they think about you. (And remember what was said about parasites farming families.)

As you listen to and address the concerns of the various aspects of self within you, it will get more and more quiet in your mind. You'll be able to hear whispers from the Great Spirit that are intended for your ears only. You'll feel so much less anxiety as you clear your field of other people's energy, and help your younger selves to let go of the past. Peace and clarity are excellent reasons to dedicate yourself to this work.

♥

Bringing Unconditional Love to Conditional Relationships

Patterns of the 'silent treatment', bullying, name calling, and hurtful actions behind my back are some of the things that I've been grappling with in my family of origin. It's a paradigm that many lightworkers and star seeds are facing in our relationships.

We are meant to bring unconditional love to these hurtful dynamics. But how? The answer is always in the higher dimensions, and rarely in the 3rd dimension. Here are some quick tips that take a while to unpack and integrate:

- The work on Earth at this time for lightworkers and star seeds is self-mastery. Stop expecting everything to be lovey dovey and light-filled. YOU bring the light to the darkness. That's the job.

- Very likely, your soul is older and has more mastery in love than the ones with whom you have difficult relationship dynamics. For example, you might be an old soul daughter born to a younger soul mother. You might have felt your whole life like you were the one teaching when you felt it should have been the other way around. This is by soul agreement. And although it's uncomfortable, it's in right relationship. Stop arguing with the agreement you made to teach your (younger soul) parent about unconditional love by being their child, and release your resentments. Work on self-mastery.

- Your 3rd dimensional identity does not have the grace to forgive trespasses and fill up the hole inside from not receiving love from conditional love relationships. You must lift your self-identification beyond the temporal 3rd dimension into the higher dimensions of soul, and connect with that which is bigger than you to fill up the love tank. From soul identity, you can forgive it because you know who you are in truth and see the bigger picture. *(This does not mean spiritual bypassing your feelings in the 3rd dimension.)*

- Leverage your power as an older soul to direct the flow of energy in your relationships. Be mindful of the stories you tell because those influence 3rd dimensional reality. Practice self-mastery to not be hooked by low-vibrational behaviors of others...do not ignore it, and do not engage it. Be aware of the totality while redirecting attention where you want it to go. Become the master of co-creating reality and elevating consciousness on the planet.

For this last suggestion, I want to share an experience I had in a small town in Peru before heading into the jungle. I was with my fellow journeyers in the town square blowing mapacho on each other to cleanse our energy fields and preparing ourselves for the jungle trip. I had never been on this excursion before, and so it was all new for me. I was taking in the sights when I saw a woman walking with big balloons under her skirt where her bottom would be. As she walked, the balloons bounced up and down. She was dressed flagrantly for attention and definitely hooked mine. Upon seeing this, my fellow travelers urgently cautioned me to release all of my attention from this woman and bring it back to our group under cover of mapacho. Apparently, she was a sorceress.

The person in your life overcome by 3rd dimensional density is no different than a sorcerer. All of their behavior is designed to hook your attention so that you will 'feed them' with the energy cord created from your attention. Many times the behaviors are designed to provoke reactions of anger, fear, and grief within you which becomes 'food' sent across the energy cord to the sorcerer. Even though many of these people are unaware of the sorcery and energy vampirism, it is still operating under the same principles. You must consciously unhook yourself from it.

The solution does not lie in ignoring the situation or walling it off or shrinking and hiding from it. The solution lies in full presence to the dynamic, keeping it in your peripheral vision without engaging it, and bringing the light of your consciousness to lift the entire spectrum at once. Shamans demonstrate this principle well when they conduct healings during ceremony. They sing songs to capture your attention on a high vibrational energy while under cover of the song they clear your low vibrational patterns with tobacco and feathers. They hold the highest truth which allows them to easily clear the lies from your field. Everything that is not love is an illusion and a lie, and it has no power in the full presence of love. It's your attention to love over illusion that is the self-mastery here.

♥

Fifth Dimensional Conversations

If you have tried to explain your awakening to someone who has not yet reached that point in their consciousness, you know how frustrating it can be to try to get your messages across. It can feel like every word you speak is misinterpreted and causes more frustration and less communication. It's like speaking French and expecting someone who only speaks English to understand what you're saying. Speaking louder only serves to increase the frustration levels of the person with whom you are trying to bridge. When people lodged in Personality notice that you've got an expanded consciousness they can feel like you're being arrogant; but really this is their own insecurity and self-judgement because their Soul knows you know something they don't yet know that is really vital and important, and this triggers the 'not enough' feelings in the Personality. It's like being in a math class where you understand how to solve the problem and got an A, but your friend cannot yet figure out the math and is feeling demoralized. Something has to 'click' and until it does, there's not much you can do besides be supportive that your friend will eventually have the lightbulb go off.

If someone in your life is extremely resistant to what you are saying— perhaps because your evolution is requiring them to change—then it can generate a lot of toxic energy to keep pushing your understanding on the other person. Do not be surprised if resistant family members try to pull you back down into the historical paradigm through ridicule, shaming, withholding love, bullying, or other forms of family betrayal. Resist the urge to judge the behavior; it is likely motivated by fear. Heal your inner voices that are wounded by this behavior, and claim your sovereignty. Any place you are relying on family for your self-love or validation or resource is an area that will be challenged as you ascend your consciousness. Rather than be upset about the challenges as they arise, see them as part of the process of becoming sovereign and ascending consciousness.

You are invited to see these challenges as opportunities to test your psychic skills as well. While it can be very difficult to talk 'sense' to a crusty person whose mind is controlled by the Personality, it is much easier to communicate psychically to the Soul. How can you do this? By bringing the conversation to the Fifth Dimension.

To do this, open sacred space to create a clear channel of communication of the highest vibration. Then imagine a familiar yet neutral setting where you can have a conversation with the other person's Soul. Invite the person to listen to what you have to say, and then give the Soul a chance to respond. You can ask very direct questions of the other person's Soul, and then listen with neutrality to the answer. You are here with a spirit of curiosity to gain more information that might be helpful for you in the Third Dimension as you interact with this person. You cannot 'control' anyone from the Fifth Dimension, and should not use this medium for manipulation. You can simply state your case and receive honest feedback much more easily.

Another way to do this is to use a pen and paper as suggested in the last section. Invite the other person's Soul to a conversation on your paper, ask a question, then write the answer using autonomic writing. Debbie Lynn Grace recommends to actually change seats when you write from the other person's Soul, and then back to your seat to respond from yourself. What you are actually doing in this process is channeling their Soul, so you want to keep the boundaries clear by having a different space for them to 'sit' than your physical body. You can also use a stone to anchor their Soul into the physical for the purpose of the conversation. The stone in this case just maintains the frequency of the Soul with which you want to communicate. It doesn't affect the other person at all because everyone is sovereign. The stone acts like a telephone.

Warning: If your channel is muddy, the Personality can interfere with the signal you receive from the other person's Soul. So please do not take the information you receive as 100% accurate. Realize the power of your Personality to influence what you hear and see from the other person. If the information is balanced, and you are receiving information that reflects the responsibility you hold in the relationship, then it is most likely close to the truth. It's a starting point for understanding the other person's perspective.

The information and resolution you receive in the Fifth Dimensional conversation can be gently introduced now in the Third Dimension using your empathy skills, keeping in mind the other person's Personality may not be aware of the Soul-level conversation you had. While people are awakening on the planet, it's respectful to not mention that you're having Fifth Dimensional conversations with someone who is lodged in Personality because it can make people feel manipulated and at a disadvantage because they don't currently have this capability. So please use this respectfully and responsibly.

Do not misuse this technique as a way to yell or argue with the other person. That is psychic attack. It is also psychic attack to visualize and intend harm towards another person with anger and hostility, or to put someone's picture on a punching bag and punch it. I've heard of an anger management coach that gave this homework to a client. **This is psychic attack.** Do not misuse the Fifth Dimension in this way. Use Fifth Dimensional conversations to create greater harmony, peace, and understanding. Any misuse of power will result in negative karma on your Soul so it behooves you to be responsible. Once you know better, you have to do better.

People who are stuck in the Personality frequently attack others psychically without knowing they are doing it. If you find yourself to be a target for this kind of attack, be sure to clear your energy field of arrows and barbs that were sent your way. Also be sure to regularly remove energetic cords with people who are siphoning your energy or infecting your energy field with their toxic emotions.

We are human, so if you find yourself projecting anger or hostility toward another person, simply do the work to release and restore the energy. Ho'Oponopono is a wonderful prayer:

I'm sorry. Please forgive me. Thank you. I love you.

Repeat it until you feel the energy has cleared.

♥

Gratitude

Bring yourself to a feeling of gratitude every day, and then express your gratitude towards the Earth and all her allies. Express your gratitude towards your ancestors and all of your relations. Express your gratitude towards your partner, children, friends, and colleagues. The energy and intention of gratitude uplifts the vibration, and so you can be an instrument of evolution!

Years ago during a meditation I saw a very specific practice of sending gratitude and love to the Earth. It's simple. Feel how grateful you are for the Earth for all she provides in your life, and then place both of your palms flat upon her belly and send love and gratitude from your heart through your heart meridians, down your arms and through your hands into the Earth. This energy will recycle back to you in your life in bountiful ways.

The Q'ero send gratitude every day to the apus, especially Ausangatay the Holy Mountain. The Huichol send gratitude every day to Quemado, the Holy Mountain. I send gratitude every day when opening sacred space for all of my allies. In this way, you keep your relationships healthy and strong with a constant pulse of love and gratitude.

Gratitude is one of our most powerful tools for building New Earth.

♥

Remember Your Unique Thumbprint

As you can imagine, I felt somewhat daunted by the task of bringing all the messages within this book out into the world in a clear, concise way that could build a bridge to many different people operating from diverse perspectives about life, spirituality and 'God'. After a powerful prayer session to the Great Spirit to help me condense the teachings into a single undeniable truth, what I received is something obvious. And it seems that truth is often right in front of us in the simple things we overlook.

Here is what I wrote in my journal that day:

I was born with a mark that is symbolic of a journey that is universal, yet personal and deeply sacred. The mark is the Creator's reminder that I was created intentionally with love and walking a path that only I am designed to walk. Every single one of us is gifted a unique mark for a unique life. The mark is placed on our thumbs to make it easy to remember.

What I have come to understand is that each body is like a thumbprint suit that the soul slips on for a one-time exploration of the loops and spirals of that unique pathway through life.

You're the only one inside your thumbprint suit. No one can truly understand what you're perceiving, experiencing, and knowing because they're not in your thumbprint suit…you are. This makes it clear why it's preposterous to look to other people for the answers that only you can find. We can only walk a few miles together along the journey of life, or intersect for moments of collaborative-knowing which are truly enjoyable moments…to be understood by another. Ultimately, however, the design of your thumbprint suit will lead you where YOU need to go to fully immerse in the unique experience you are meant to have.

If you do not fully explore and understand and love your thumbprint of a life…no one ever will. It's up to you.

♥

And now let me introduce my friend Jennifer Hough who is going to share with you the science behind awakening. Jennifer Hough is a seer, alchemist, author and Facilitator of Awakening. Her ability to 'see' people holographically evolved as a result of running one of the largest Holistic Nutrition Clinics in Canada (The Vital You) from 1994 until now. That ability evolved from medical intuition such that she could witness individual lives, histories, and the collective societal status in holographic form. Jennifer founded *The Wide Awakening* in 2008 to assist us all to remember more deeply the reason we are here, based on the information that she sees and continues to evolve. Her mission is to shine a light within us, so we can all bring Heaven with us wherever we go! Her flagship program *Get Out of Your Own Way*™ incorporates online workshops and in-person retreats.

The Science Behind an Exponential Awakening Shift for Humanity by Jennifer Hough

On many occasions I have been asked *"Why do you have so much inspired energy, when there seems to be many things wrong with this world, politics, economics, healthcare and even within my own life? What are you seeing that I don't?"* It's a great question that I think is worthy of a powerful answer. For me the answer lies in the realm of physics, and some advancements in awareness that support the idea of making quantum leaps instead of getting linear results. It's all about building metaphysical bridges that transcend our known way we do things. I find bridge building to be such an essential tool, that I have spent the rest of my life teaching others how to master that skill. But I digress, it's important to get a context for how I came to the science of spiritual awakening first.

Let's be clear, I grew up in a very linear world. My Mother was a teacher and my Dad is and was an entrepreneur. I went to school, got straight A's (in response to trying to be worthy and approved of by my Dad), was painfully shy, had acne, wore glasses, stayed away from people, put my nose down and went to University of Waterloo for Accounting and Economics. So my background education was neither exceptional, scientific, nor was it spiritual in the traditional or new age-y sense. That worked to my advantage, and I find it works to most peoples' advantage because much like myself, we end up using our instincts instead of our heads when it comes to making sense of the world. I find myself approaching the marriage of spirituality and science with a child-like curiosity, versus the seriousness of someone trying to get it right. I recommend that as you read further, you take the same approach of child-like curiosity and wonder. That's where the non-linear 'aha's live, after all.

I have always questioned God/Creation/Spirit about the crazy uncomfortable things that seem to happen on this planet. Even at 3 years old, I thought adults were doing it all the hard way. I remember standing in front of the television beside my father at 17 years old, watching some seemingly challenging war in the Middle East and knowing that the contrast did not have to be so disturbing. I didn't know how I knew that we could find a way to more harmony with ourselves and others, but my father, in his protective way, assured me that it's none of my business and to keep my head down and study. I don't do well when people tell me what to do.

As a result, I have travelled to distant lands and mystics to explore spiritual awakening. Mosques in Jerusalem, Temples in Toronto, Catholic Church in Montreal, Hindu Temples in Bali and India, Stone Circles in Ireland and England, Pyramids, Bahai ceremony in California, played with Kahuna's in Hawaii and Ayahuasca journeys in Peru and the middle of the Amazon in Ecuador and so many more. The experiences have been humbling to say the least. More importantly each of these experiences added to my passion to find the commonalities within our understandings of the world. Why were so many of these masters filled with passion and energy to teach and share possibility despite the overwhelming evidence of suffering in the world?

I found no scientific proof for anything they taught me. But I yearned for it. So unconsciously, I launched a profound request into 'the field', as Kerri would say "to the Great Spirit". The answers started pouring in during my early 30's and continue today, in the form of scientific studies, serendipitous meetings with physicists, and wakened dreams that showed me where to look for my answers. Little did I know I was not the only one looking to marry my deep instinctual knowing with science, let alone learn how to embody that knowing so I could live it and pass it on to others.

So here is my answer to the question that so many of my students and staff have asked. *"How can science possibly support a case for our awakening? What in Physics supports being hopeful and even inspired in such a harsh world?"* Here are some of the things that I have found.

Keep in mind that much of what I am sharing was first experienced through my wakened dream state and then backed up by studies, many of which have been coming out over the past few years. Some information I am sharing is my best interpretation of what I've been shown, combined with years of experience and personal evidence in my life and the lives of 100,000's of others we have worked with around the world. This is the case for awakening, as well as a case for how the world can shift in an *instant*........ This is about the science in support of your life as a new book (the book of Destiny), not a new chapter in the old book of Fate.

PHOTONS AND HUMANS

Physicists Bohr, Wigner, Wheeler and more were brave enough to start to understand the nature of photons. I did not realize prior to understanding what some of these great thinkers had to say, that photons played such a major part in our every day. My first foray into the idea of photons started when I could feel the past, decisions and incongruences within my clients and the connection each of these things had, to their health issues. Some thought I was medically intuitive, but what did that mean? I wanted a real explanation. First I found studies from Germany and Russia that showed that light particles/photons (not photosynthesis by the way) travelled to and from plants constantly. Recently there are more studies that show that our cells are giving off and receiving photons and I could see that masses of information about us—our journeys and who we are— were being communicated to and from us. I realized that this was the scientific explanation for intuition, instinct, medical intuition, horse whispering and any kind of communication that transcended needing ears. Our cells are ears, and there are trillions of them. Imagine how important Creation must hold the idea of communing with metaphysical information if we only have two ears to hear versus trillions of cells to take in information.

From the MIT Technology review in 2010: "It looks very much as if many cells use light to communicate."

For me the most important idea that came from this realization about photons, is that as we change/heal/awaken, the information that caused us to be able to evolve, is now available to everyone. Photons carry that information. Remember that photon packages of light travel around the world 7 times in a second, and you and I are made of sender/receivers of that information. We truly are all in this together.

THE FABRIC OF OUR EXISTENCE

Here are some terms various scientific and spiritual people use for Dark Matter: cosmic super fluid, unseen gravity or cosmic environment. Regardless, this unseen gravity comprises between 68% and 93% of all that exists (depending on which scientist you ask). Consider the metaphor that the 'cosmic super fluid' is water, and we are a sponge. The water is through us, affecting us, around us and we are wet with it. If Atoms are the substance of 3 Dimensions, we are the creative force with our dreams and goals that bridge other dimensions with 3D, and photons are the substance of other dimensional aspects of us that can become 3D, then Dark Matter is the swimming pool in which it all co-conspires to become. This 'swimming pool' environment creates the space for Photons to gather and go from multi-D to 3D. Much like the fluid and nutrients in the womb provide what is needed for creating a baby. Sperms and eggs (Humans and Photons) hold the potential of becoming a baby given certain environmental conditions. Imagine that those conditions are

1. Our magnetics: how we feel and the frequency we emanate and our availability for a baby based on our stress levels.
2. The unseen gravity, or the cosmic environment is that fabric that supports our thought, life and imagination babies.
3. The physical environment including moon cycles, nutrients and hormones and finally...

4. The alignment with our overall path/intention and dreams as a human being.

Imagine that in this environment things don't happen linearly, they happen by finding the most direct route. Here, there is no being constrained by time, space or history. The beautiful part about being able to experience this realm of existence is that I started to realize that we literally know almost nothing about how magical life can become. When I embraced this idea, and knew it to be true, I became a receiver of non-linear results that had me laughing out loud with glee. Imagine what would happen if you knew you didn't have to control your environment, and that the entire fabric of your existence was in support of the most direct route to your dreams and fulfillment. How would you spend your time?

FRACTALS

In a nutshell, fractals have to do with never ending patterns. It's one of the ways that scientists have tried to describe the Universe. The problem is that as I have been shown, although fractals or patterns pervade all systems, they are just a part of the systems, not the whole thing. One day I was in communication with greater wisdom, and was shown that from the grandest view of existence, we are all part of a mass pattern at one level, but every part of the pattern reflects the whole. For instance: in Chinese medicine the tongue reflects all of the organs, in Reflexology you can find them all in the feet and hands, and in Iridology, different parts of the eye reflect the health of different glands, organs and systems in the body. Even Dr. Ryke Geerde Hamer discovered that you could find lesions in the brain using CAT Scans that reflect the patterns of behavior that come from earlier trauma. He demonstrated that if you change the pattern of trauma, you change the lesion in the CAT Scan and you change that person's life. Pattern, pattern, pattern. Imagine in this scenario that I am a molecule of water in the ocean, and that if I move, I then move the entire ocean by logical inference. This is what I saw about our world. If you change, I now have the opportunity to change. If you create a new way of breaking free from pain, that 'way' (or bridge) now exists in our collective experience pattern, and it is now a part of every pattern. If one aspect of consciousness changes, all aspects must include that change immediately. It becomes available to all of us. All it takes is a little consciousness to be aware that all of the solutions are all around us. Nature is the most pervasive example of the relentlessness of Creation to show us our abundant nature...we are swimming in the pattern of the generosity and abundance of trees and plants and they don't judge as they breathe out what we breathe in. In noticing that pattern, we can bring that awareness into our bodies, and heal. In healing, a new pattern is available for all humanity.

MULTI-DIMENSIONAL DNA

Geneticists from around the world are starting to understand that junk DNA is not junk at all. The problem with science is that we can only understand it from the perspective of the measurement tools we have. It's like trying to look at an electron through a Doctor's microscope. Of course you will have a hard time believing that electrons exist: you don't have an electron microscope. What has become blatantly obvious to me after an awakened dream in 2007, is that we have characteristics and sensory devices that operate beyond 3D. We are intuitive, we predict things, we collapse time when we have a deja vu, we seem to know what our dog is thinking, some see light around people, some see orbs of light, some bring through wisdom that there is no explanation for. I wanted to explain why I could 'see' my clients beyond 3D, even though I did not have the right equipment in 3D to view the explanation, or so it would seem. Then I was shown a very rational explanation. It takes 3D DNA to give us our 3D senses, so what kind of DNA does it take to have the senses I described above? Well, if they are multi-dimensional senses, it only makes sense that there is metaphysical machinery in place to connect through our 'cosmic gravity', and instruct the photons to upgrade our abilities. Consider again, that junk DNA only seems that way because we cannot measure nor see the mechanism in place, because we don't have the tools. Just use your logic. Of course, in order to have abilities beyond 3D, you need mechanisms and conduits from the realms where those abilities live and breathe.

Imagine that those abilities (I call them Innate Abilities of which there are 24 fundamentals) could be embodied in 3D. My experience of people that embody these abilities, including myself, is that there is exponentially less struggle as it would appear that when we use these abilities we have the capacity to flow outside of the linear models of getting things done.

EVERYTHING IS MOVING FORWARD AND OUT FUELED BY BOTH THE YEARNING FOR MORE HARMONY AND concurrently CATALYZED BY THE LACK OF IT

Time to bring it all together and answer the question that so many have asked of me, and I had asked of Creation. How can there be hope in times of great change? Because there are guidelines and laws about the way physics works.

1. As we become more conscious, so does everyone else at an exponential rate. Fractal theory supports that. The biophoton operating system in humans makes way for that.

2. We are swimming in the soup of harmony, as the entire Universe operates from a place of harmonic non-resistant flow. At the core of our being we are made of that fabric and it is constantly calling us home to fluidity.

3. The super-powers that are connected to our Junk DNA, allow us to make non-linear results. However, they also allow us to create new systems of operation so that we upgrade HOW WE DO THINGS. That means that we are also upgrading the speed at which we can shift. The cool thing is that anyone operating from greed, fear or power is not present to the skills to thrive, because they are operating from survival.

4. Every event that happens in our lives either reminds us of what we love, or catalyzes us towards a life we would love. Either way, over time, all tends towards more creativity and love, not less. The more sensitive to fluidity we become (and the ones being born right now are definitely sensitized to incongruent behaviors around them) the less large spikes in drama will be tolerated.

That is the beauty of embodying those Innate Abilities. One also becomes far more creative, witness the so called Millennials who are becoming millionaires, causing shifts and changing the world at a pace that far outdoes the generations before them. More sensitive, more embodied.

The bottom line is that we are just learning to drive this Ferrari. I remember five times in my life where Great Spirit (Infinite Wisdom/All that IS/Greater Consciousness) emphatically showed me versions of what is possible for us as a race and as individuals. Each experience had its purpose in my awakening. One happened in my twenties, at the beginning of my current journey, where I was guided to walk a girl who lived on the streets to the psych ward. Her story brought me to my knees in tears in the middle of Toronto as I realized that she represented millions of children all over the world that suffered at the hands of their parents. I looked up and asked *'Why would you show me this....I can't save the world, I won't shut my feelings off and I refuse to become a martyr.'* It was in the answer I received that I realized that there is no question or problem that does not have a solution. The answer I got back from my Cosmic Entourage was this:

"In a world of no space and time, as you heal yourself, learn to love your life, apply your super-powers to fulfilling projects and teach others...those both the future and past will have all of the information that is needed for heaven to expand. Show up for the life you were born to, jump in with passion. Allow yourself to be fueled by inspiration and catalyzed by struggle and pain. If there can be a problem, there is instantly a solution in physics. Line up with the answers and be grateful for the opportunity to create. Your passion is a 3 Dimensional and Metaphysical delivery system. Use it, cherish it, honor it. Remember that in our world, there is no time…and you do not die. You are on an infinite co-creative ride. You just keep coming back for the ride. How much love can you emanate on this ride? If you play that game, your life will be blessed, and in return so will the lives of many others retroactively and for all time. "

I'm incredibly blessed to have been catalyzed to this work. I also know that in my showing up for what is asked of me with reverence, joy and grace, that same journey is available to all. The same is true for your life. Your life matters in this multi-dimensional world and on this planet.

"Your life will become someone else's stepping stones to the light. Live it fully." – Jennifer Hough

♥

Quotes

"Nobody is superior, nobody is inferior, but nobody is equal either. People are simply unique, incomparable. You are you, I am I." — Rajneesh

"To be beautiful means to be yourself. You don't need to be accepted by others. You need to accept yourself. When you are born a lotus flower, be a beautiful lotus flower, don't try to be a magnolia flower. If you crave acceptance and recognition and try to change yourself to fit what other people want you to be, you will suffer all your life. True happiness and true power lie in understanding yourself, accepting yourself, having confidence in yourself."
—Nhat Hanh

"If you think you are too small to make a difference, try sleeping with a mosquito." — Dalai Lama

"If you are kind, people may accuse you of selfish, ulterior motives: Be kind anyway. If you are successful you will win some false friends and true enemies: Succeed anyway. If you are honest and frank people will try to cheat you: Be honest anyway. What you spend years building, someone could destroy overnight: Build anyway. If you find serenity and happiness, they may be jealous of you: Be happy anyway. The good you do today, will often be forgotten by tomorrow: Do good anyway. Give the world the best you have, and it may never be enough: Give your best anyway." — Mother Teresa

"Many people, especially ignorant people, want to punish you for speaking the truth, for being correct, for being you. Never apologize for being correct, or for being years ahead of your time. If you're right and you know it, speak your mind. Speak your mind. Even if you are a minority of one, the truth is still the truth." — Mahatma Ghandi

Reminders To Yourself

I am a unique thumbprint.
There never was, and never will be, anyone like me.
It is my privilege to discover and experience my unique life journey.

A Courageous Heart

"With an undefended heart, we can fall in love with life over and over every day. We can become children of wonder, grateful to be walking on earth, grateful to belong with each other and to all of creation. We can find our true refuge in every moment, in every breath." - Tara Brach

For weeks before publishing this book I had been exploring the idea of the undefended heart. This exploration led me to the conclusion that an undefended heart is an open heart, full of love, that breathes free and safe in the world without the need to guard itself from attack, prove its worthiness, apologize for itself, or defend its territory. But what did that really mean?

Simultaneously, I was conceiving of a brand for my firewalk events to inspire people to be in community with one another. What was resonating very strongly was this image I had used for event promotion that had a lion with flames for a mane that was roaring and on fire. I had called the event "Courageous Heart Firewalk Transformation." People loved it.

Then one morning as I opened sacred space under my favorite trees, I had a powerful experience. It was a beautiful day in May, partly cloudy sky after days of rain. As I faced the trees to the South, I was contemplating my new inspiration to create the Courageous Heart Firewalks. I was visualizing a powerful image of a lion whose mane was on fire, and the flames formed a heart around his face. It was a feeling of fierceness and protection and courage and love.

Suddenly a blue jay began swooping down around my head. It made several passes. I looked up trying to figure out why, and saw it had a nest about 8 feet above my head. I assumed that perhaps it had baby eggs or chicks in the nest that it was protecting. I asked the Winds of the South to help it feel safe with my presence, and continued with my visualization and prayers for a strong supportive container for the firewalks.

As I faced the West, the blue jay continued its attack, swooping closer and closer to my head as it passed over. A very clear message to back off. I wondered if this was a test to stand my ground? This spot had been my place to pray and open the directions for years now. It was my sacred space. I did not want to have to move. I kept praying to the West to clear fear and anything in my field that was blocking my success with my firewalks. The blue jay kept swooping and warning me away from his territory which was making it very difficult to concentrate on my prayers. I was feeling intimidated and getting a bit irritated, and even contemplated swatting at the blue jay the next time it made a pass at me.

Then I faced the north and began calling in the ancestors and lineages. The air expanded in the way it does when the Great Spirit is fully present in the spaciousness. And this is when I had one of the most profound realizations of my life. In my body I was infusing my brand with ferocity to create protection for all those who became part of the community of Courageous Heart; to make it safe for them to be courageous and face their fears and open their hearts.

In a flash I understood that summoning protection in this way was actually from fear and lack of trust that we were already safe in love. I understood that my own fear and feeling needful of protection was what caused a reaction in the blue jay to defend his territory. He was simply responding to my energy. When I faced the north direction everything changed and the blue jay went away. My heart melted into love, and I remembered that I was safe always, and since my energy changed, the blue jay no longer felt threatened.

This awareness deepened within me in the most profound way, and led me to understand that life on Earth was responding to the state of the human consciousness around it. Lions were fierce if they felt they had to defend themselves from attack, but otherwise could be very peaceful. It's the energy of our human consciousness that is impacting all of life on Earth. If we are at war with ourselves, the planet is at war with itself, because we influence everything around us. And as I wrote this sentence, a dove flew to sit on my front porch steps and looked at me and cooed.

I remember being in the jungle with the Shipibo not too long ago. There was a giant black spider with white markings on its back that I was told was poisonous and could jump 4 feet. It seemed that spider was always where I needed to go: on the door into the maloka, on the toilet paper roll on the way to my tent, on the rafter above my head. It was everywhere and I was afraid of it. On the last day it tried to get into my bag as I was packing. The shaman's grandson came over to help when he heard me squeal. He simply moved toward the spider gently and it retreated to the wall. "The spider is my friend," he said.

If you bring the energy of fear into your life, the world around you will respond with fear.

If you bring the energy of love into your life, the world around you will respond with love.

This is way beyond a personal revolution when you really get this. All of life on Earth is waiting for us humans to bring the energy of love into the third dimensional experience of Earth, so that that all of life on Earth can flourish in love. For us to really bring the energy of love to the Earth, we have to wake up to realize that the Great Spirit loves and cherishes every single creation equally. There is no creation that is less than another, and there are no mistakes. Everything is created with a purpose. Everything has its own 'medicine' to share. Everything is a part of the greater consciousness called the Great Spirit. Every rock, every tree, every mountain, every stream, every insect, every animal, every bird...everything.

When you understand that everything has its own unique medicine to bring, you can honor it rather than fear it. And you can begin to put yourself into right relationship with all that is by dismantling notions of superiority and separation, and listening to the larger force that moves around and through you. The Q'ero shamans call this being in ayne. There's a bigger picture and you can align yourself to it by intentionally stepping out of collective agreement to human insanity and courageously taking the actions that the Great Spirit inspires you to take.

The definition of courage is "the mental or moral strength to venture, persevere, and withstand danger, fear or difficulty." From Brene Brown:

The root of the word courage is cor - the Latin word for heart. In one of its earliest forms, the word courage meant "To speak one's mind by telling all one's heart." Over time, this definition has changed, and today, we typically associate courage with heroic and brave deeds.

All of this is true of courage. And all of it applies to a Courageous Heart.

A Courageous Heart is majestic like the lion because he is the manifestation of the Divine walking the Earth, and his knowing of this makes him strong, resilient, and powerful. A Courageous Heart is in her knowing as Love, surrendered to Love, emanating Love, from the center of her being where her Divine Spark guides the way. A Courageous Heart needs no protection because he IS the protection by being the vibration of Love on Earth, and so a Courageous Heart lets down her armor and shines the light of her undefended heart. A Courageous Heart has become the medicine of Love by knowing who he is in truth, who she is in truth, and taking the inspired actions of a transparent and vulnerable heart in faith and trust.

A Courageous Heart is a stand for love in the face of fear, no matter what.

Cultivating a Courageous Heart takes some work. It requires some experiential proof that you are safe to let down your guard, and some shifts in the way you are **being** so you can show up with curiosity, centeredness and compassion.

When you know who you are in truth, and make a stand for yourself to express that truth unapologetically from a place of power within, you can show up in challenging moments with a Courageous Heart.

When you let go of convincing or proving or needing validation, and you allow your truth to stand by itself naked and vulnerable...you are showing up with a Courageous Heart.

When you reveal your naked truth and honor it despite anyone else's opinions and reactions, and you don't diminish it in the face of criticism...you are showing up with a Courageous Heart.

A Courageous Heart pulses the pure truth of your essential self through your veins...and this truth, this light, is more powerful than any attack.

It takes work to walk in the world with a Courageous Heart. You have to be mindful to not react from fear, and to move through the fear to peel back the layers and set down the armor. You have to practice self-mastery to transform fear to love. You have to listen to all of life to hear the messages from the Great Spirit that guide you along the Beauty Way.

Your personal work to tune into the Great Spirit and cultivate a Courageous Heart is invaluable because a Courageous Heart is exactly what the world needs now.

♥

Quotes

"When you are in doubt, be still, and wait;
When doubt no longer exists for you then go forward
with courage.
So long as mists envelop you, be still;
Be still until the sunlight pours through and dispels
the mists
-As it surely will.
Then act with courage."

— Ponca Chief White Eagle, Go Forward With Courage

"What you do for yourself, any gesture of kindness, any
gesture of gentleness, any gesture of honesty and clear
seeing toward yourself, will affect how you experience
the world. In fact, it will transform how you experience
the world. What you do for yourself, you're doing for
others,
and what you do for others, you're doing for yourself."
— Pema Chodron

"May I stress the need for courageous, intelligent, and
dedicated leadership... Leaders of sound integrity.
Leaders not in love with publicity, but in love with
justice. Leaders not in love with money, but in love with
humanity. Leaders who can subject their particular egos
to the greatness of the cause."
— Martin Luther King, Jr.

"Every great dream begins with a dreamer."
— Harriet Tubman

About Kerri Hummingbird Sami

Kerri Hummingbird Sami is a soul guide, shamanic energy healer, award-winning best-selling author and inspirational speaker. Kerri has over 20 years of experience in leading by inspiration, and a special passion for empowering women to be the artists of their lives. She mentors women to rewrite the story of their lives through inner transformation, connection to essence, remembrance of purpose, and realignment to authenticity and truth.

She is certified in energy medicine by the Four Winds Light Body school, certified as a spiritual coach by the Artist of the Spirit Coach Training Program and HeatherAsh Amara, certified in empowerment and firewalk training by Sundoor, and certified as a Warrior Goddess Facilitator. She is the past President of the Austin Chapter of the International Association of Women (IAW).

In 2014, The Indie Spiritual Book Awards conferred the honor of "Best in Category" to *Awakening To Me: One Woman's Journey To Self Love*, and in 2015 it won Pinnacle Best in Category for Self-Help and National Indie Excellence Awards Winner in Category for Spirituality. Her 2015 best-selling book *From We To Me: Emerging Self After Divorce*, is a best-seller. Kerri lives with the love of her life, his two children, and her two teenage sons in the Austin area. She works with clients around the world.

Prior to her career as a Soul Guide, Ms. Hummingbird had a 20-year career as a technical and marketing communications consultant in both Silicon Valley and Austin high-tech communities. She has served in leadership since she began working, most notably serving on the Board of the Silicon Valley chapter of the Society for Technical Communication. She also inspired and led over 150 artists to open their studios to the public as the Executive Director of the non-profit Silicon Valley Open Studios in the Bay Area, California for several years in the early 2000s.

Award-winning, best-selling books:

Awakening To Me: One Woman's Journey To Self Love, 2014

From We To Me: Emerging Self After Divorce, 2016

Other titles:

Reinvent Yourself: Indulge Your Deepest Desires By Becoming Who You Are Starving To Be, Available at www.kerrihummingbird.com/gift

Get An Immediate Shift

If you struggle with mental chatter, anxiety, depression, negative energy from others, or boundaries, consider this Guided Meditation Pack.

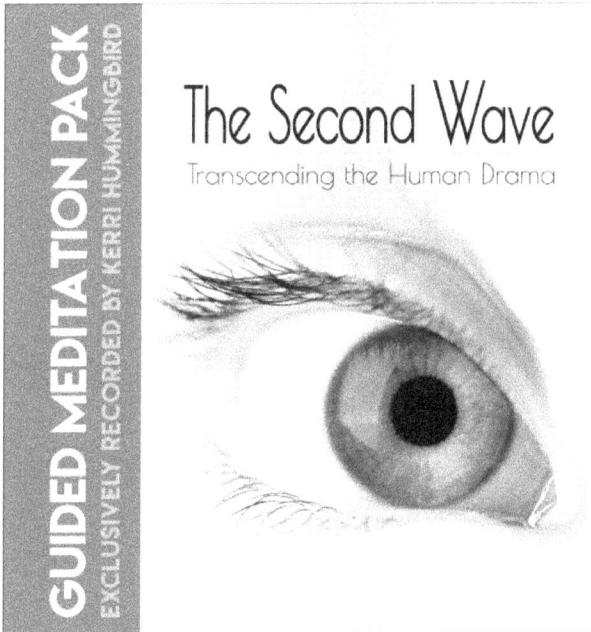

- Clear negative energy and mental chatter with a powerful 3 minute healing from Spirit of Tobacco
- Increase your confidence by grounding yourself to feel secure
- Fill Yourself Up with positive high vibration light and ascension codes to rebuild and reinforce your body's natural shield

Visit https://www.thesecondwave.media/secondwave-meditations

Receive Weekly Channeled Guidance

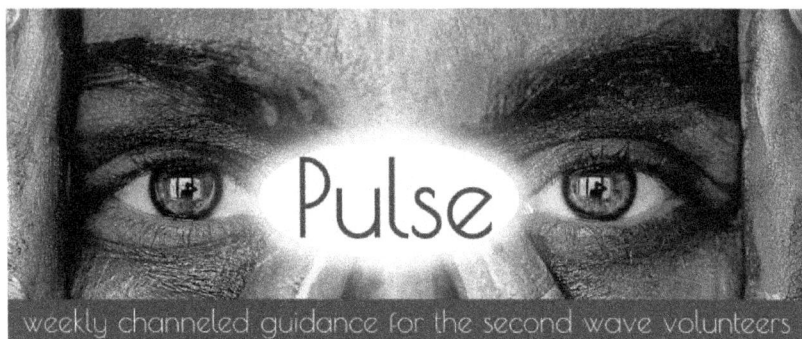

With the Second Wave Pulse, you will receive:

- The Rights of the Keeper of the Time to Come in a special meditation. This is a special rite shared with Kerri Hummingbird by the Q'ero shamans in Peru on top of Ausangatay, the Holy Mountain. It is an energetic installation designed to support Rainbow Warriors.
- 4 Sunday morning audios per month with channeled invocations, healings, guidance, rituals, and vibe-lifting energy transmissions to help you open your heart, mind, and life to the divine.
- 1 exclusive monthly LIVE Pulse call and Q/A. Receive a monthly group live healing invitation from Kerri and the guides beyond the veil. Kerri will send powerful shamanic healing transmissions AND will answer your questions on ANY topic each month.
- secret Facebook group for leaders of the Second Wave!
- 15-20% discount on courses, workshops and retreats including Second Wave Town Hall events.

Yes! I want the Pulse! $22/month: https://bit.ly/2JEubuH

Yes! I want a Year of the Pulse! $197 (25% off): https://bit.ly/2Ss4nVp

Resources

---

[1] The first time I heard of the Second Wave was through the work of Dolores Cannon. She interviewed hundreds of subjects while they were under hypnosis and asked questions of their sub-conscious self. From these sub-conscious interviews, she formed the basis of her understanding about the First Wave, Second Wave and Third Wave of volunteers to Earth. Some of the information that has channeled through me for this book is compatible with information Dolores Cannon discovered. Some of the insights are contrary to this research or expand upon it in new ways.

[2] After the book was completed, but days before it was published, White Eagle, ascended master, revealed to me that he had been guiding this publication, and my entire life. So while it is accurate to say that I channeled the information from the Great Spirit, it is also accurate to say that I channeled it from White Eagle. He did, however, enjoy the surprise.

[3] Excerpt from Awaken.com

[4] *The Gifts of Imperfection*, Brenè Brown

[5] This is a little gem of wisdom I received from Jose Stevens, and it comes in very handy.

[6] *The Four Agreements*, Don Miguel Ruiz

[7] *Courageous Dreaming: How Shamans Dream The World Into Being*, Alberto Villoldo, PhD

[8] A helpful resource for understanding Human Design Type is Chetan Parkyn: www.humandesignforusall.com

[9] This has been a very powerful message for me from Tracey Trottenberg and George Kansas

www.ingramcontent.com/pod-product-compliance
Lightning Source LLC
Chambersburg PA
CBHW030932090426
42737CB00007B/403